READING EXPERT

A 5-LEVEL READING COURSE for EFL Readers

2

READING EXPERT 2

Series Editor	Yoo-seung Shin
Project Editors	Mina Song, Hyobin Park, Yuna Kim
Writers	Patrick Ferraro, Keeran Murphy, Nathaniel Galletta
Design	Hyunah Song
Editorial Designer	In-sun Lee
Special Thanks to	Seung-pyo Han, Hoe-young Kim, Hey-won Nam

Copyright©2020 by NE Neungyule, Inc.

First Printing 5 January 2020

13th Printing 15 May 2024

ISBN   979-11-253-2928-2

Photo Credits

www.istockphoto.com
www.shutterstock.com
www.dreamstime.com
www.hellophoto.kr
www.bullittcenter.org

INTRODUCTION

Reading Expert is a five-level reading course for EFL readers, with special relevance for junior and senior high school students. They will acquire not only reading skills but also knowledge of various contemporary and academic topics.

FEATURES

Covering Current, Academic Topics: Topics ranging from real world issues to academic subjects are covered in an easy and interesting way so that junior and senior high school students can understand them. These subjects appeal to students and can hold their attention.

Expanding Knowledge: Each unit is composed of two articles under one topic heading. These articles will help students expand their knowledge of various topics, including social and academic issues.

Practicing Reading Skills: Reading comprehension checkups encourage the use of important reading skills. They can be used to evaluate and improve students' comprehension skills, such as identifying main ideas, specific details, and implied meanings.

Tackling Longer Passages: EFL junior and senior high school students often find it difficult to read long passages because they have not received much exposure to lengthy material. Interesting and well-developed passages customized for EFL students will help learners to approach longer passages with ease. Summarizing exercises will also help them understand the flow of long passages.

Test-Oriented Questions: Many comprehension checkup questions are similar to TOEFL questions. They will be a stepping stone in preparing students for English tests at school, as well as for official English language tests such as TOEFL.

LEVEL	GRADE	WORDS LIMITS	UNITS
Reading Expert 1	Low-Intermediate	230 - 270	15
Reading Expert 2	Intermediate	250 - 300	15
Reading Expert 3		270 - 330	15
Reading Expert 4	Low-Advanced	290 - 350	15
Reading Expert 5		300 - 370	15

TO THE **STUDENTS**

Why Is Reading Challenging?

It is a very challenging, sometimes painful, experience for EFL students to read English newspapers, magazines, or books. There are various reasons for this: the high level of vocabulary and sentence structure, a lack of background knowledge on the topic, and a need for certain reading skills.

Become an Expert Reader with Reading Expert!

Reading Expert is a five-level reading course that is intended to improve your reading abilities gradually. There are 4 areas of reading strategies you need to focus on to improve your reading abilities.

1. Vocabulary Skills

When you run into an unfamiliar word, try to continue reading. In many cases a couple of unfamiliar words will not prevent general understanding of a passage. If you think they are still a barrier to further reading, use context clues. If they also do not provide enough information, it will be necessary to use your Word Book or look up the "problem word" in a dictionary.

2. Paragraph Approach

A passage is a collection of paragraphs, and the main point of each paragraph is organized into the main idea of the passage. When you read a passage, try not to just focus on the meaning of each sentence: Keep asking yourself, "What is the main point of this paragraph?" Questions on the main point of a paragraph and summary exercises will help you stay focused.

3. Understanding Long Passages

Young EFL readers have often not been exposed to long passages (more than 200 words), and they may find such passages difficult to understand. Various reading skills will be needed to understand long passages: scanning, skimming, understanding the structure of the passage, etc. Reading comprehension questions and summary exercises cover these reading skills.

4. Knowledge of the Topic

Just like when you're reading in your native language, a lack of background knowledge can prevent you from understanding the topic. The Reading Expert course covers a variety of topics, including academic subjects, social issues, world culture, and more. If you are not familiar with the topic in question, try to search for relevant information in books or on the Internet.

TO THE **TEACHER**

Reading Expert is a five-level reading course written by EFL teachers who have years of experience in teaching EFL students. It is simple to use in a classroom and interesting enough to keep students' attention. Each level is composed of 15 units, and each unit has two readings. Each unit contains the following sections:

Before Reading

The WARM-UP QUESTION before each reading is intended to get students ready by relating the topic to their lives. You can also help students by introducing background knowledge or explaining difficult words.

Readings

There are two readings for every unit. Before having students read the text, explain to them some important reading skills, such as scanning and skimming. After reading the passage, they can listen to an MP3 audio recording. Each reading is followed by a WORD CHECK. Students can use this section to practice guessing the meanings of the key words and expressions in context. WORD FOCUS, which shows collocations, synonyms, and antonyms, is provided alongside the passages. It will familiarize students with some natural English expressions while increasing their range of English vocabulary.

Comprehension Checkups

Readings are also followed by comprehension checkup questions. These are intended to help students identify the MAIN IDEA or subject of the passage and understand DETAILS. Questions related to reading skills are sometimes included.

Summary

A SUMMARY is provided for each reading and it can take a number of different forms, such as a basic summary, a graphic organizer, a note-taking summary, etc. All of these forms are designed to improve students' ability to understand and summarize a passage. There are various ways to use this section, such as assigning it as homework or having the students complete it without referring to the reading. It tests whether students understand the text as a whole.

Word Review Test

Learning vocabulary is important for EFL readers. They need to review key words, expressions, and difficult or unfamiliar words. A WORD REVIEW TEST comes at the end of every two units and is intended to test students' vocabulary.

TABLE OF **CONTENTS**

UNIT 01

Sports

READING 1

If you plan to learn a martial art, how about capoeira? Capoeira is a Brazilian art form that combines dance, music, and martial arts. Participants perform inside a circle of people who clap, sing, and play musical instruments.
5 They punch and kick without hitting each other, creating a fascinating dance. When I first began to learn capoeira, I was most impressed by its powerful actions and graceful moves. Later, however, I began to understand that it also has
10 a rich and interesting history.

It was created by slaves brought to Brazil from Africa, mostly during the 16th century. ⓐ They wanted to teach one another how to fight, but they had to hide this activity from their masters. ⓑ Therefore, they disguised it as a form of dance. ⓒ In
15 the past, this was done to indicate that the master was approaching and to warn the performers to switch from fighting moves to dance moves. ⓓ

During the Paraguayan War, which took place from 1865 to 1870, many slaves were forced to join the army. Their capoeira skills made them fierce fighters, and the art form gained many admirers. However, in 1890, shortly after slavery in Brazil was
20 ended, the government made capoeira illegal. They feared that it could be used for violent crimes. The ban on capoeira was lifted in the 1930s, and today it is one of Brazil's national sports and it is more popular than ever.

Capoeira is a beautiful art form to watch, and it is fun to participate in. What's more, it builds strength, increases flexibility, and makes you a more disciplined person.
25 I strongly encourage all of you to give capoeira a try.

‹ ●●● 03 ●● ›

WORD CHECK

Choose the correct words for the blanks from the highlighted words in the passage.

1. _____ to change sth so it is unrecognizable
2. _____ obeying rules or behaving in a controlled way
3. _____ strong and frightening
4. _____ the system of owning other people as property
5. _____ done in an attractive and elegant way

*sb: somebody / sth: something

MAIN IDEA

1 What is the passage mainly about?

a. the reason slavery was ended in Brazil
b. an art form developed by slaves in Brazil
c. a new musical style developed during a war
d. the link between Brazilian music and African dance

READING SKILL

Skimming

Skimming is looking quickly through the text to get a general idea of what it is about. We move our eyes quickly through the whole text identifying the purpose of the passage or the main idea.

DETAILS

2 Where would the following sentence best fit in paragraph 2?

> If you watch a capoeira performance today, you may notice how the musicians often change their tempo.

3 Why did the Brazilian government prohibit capoeira according to paragraph 3?

_____

4 Which is closest in meaning to <u>lifted</u>?

a. raised   b. removed   c. introduced   d. tightened

5 Which of the following is NOT true according to the passage?

a. The movements in capoeira include punching and kicking.
b. Slaves played a major role in the development of capoeira.
c. Capoeira was forbidden from being practiced during the Paraguayan War.
d. Capoeira is recommended for people who want to be both strong and flexible.

SUMMARY

6 Use the words in the box to fill in the blanks.

> sang   disguise   crime   combination   developed   banned   gain

Capoeira is a _____ of dance, music, and martial arts. African slaves who had been brought to Brazil first _____ it in the 16th century. They wanted to teach one another how to fight. However, they had to _____ this activity as a dance. After slaves successfully used it in the Paraguayan war, capoeira became popular. It was temporarily _____, but it is now more popular than ever.

Climbing the world's tallest mountains is no easy task. But it is even more difficult when it is done in what is known as "alpine style." This is what Reinhold Messner and Peter Habeler decided to do in 1975.

The alpine style of climbing was developed as an alternative to the traditional way the tall mountains of the Asian Himalayas were being climbed. In the traditional or siege style, climbers would hire dozens of assistants to set up a series of camps equipped with the necessary supplies. They would then climb their way from one camp to the next, eventually reaching the mountain's top.

But alpine style means climbing the mountain in a single attempt, carrying everything you need on your back. Named after the Alps mountain range of Europe, this style requires climbers to start at the very bottom of the mountain. They cannot use fixed ropes, bring along oxygen tanks, or hire porters to help carry their equipment and supplies.

When Messner and Habeler set out to climb the Himalayan mountain known as Gasherbrum I in this way, other climbers thought they were crazy. They thought that alpine style was fine for smaller mountains, but not the Himalayas. However, Messner and Habeler proved everyone wrong. It took them only three days to reach the top of Gasherbrum I, and they became the first ever to climb a mountain taller than 8,000 meters in the alpine style.

Despite the high risk, there are several advantages to the alpine style. Since it takes less time, there is a smaller **chance** of being caught in a snowstorm or an *avalanche. It is also better for the environment. In traditional-style expeditions, large climbing teams with many camps leave behind a lot of garbage, such as torn tents and empty oxygen tanks. But alpine-style climbers work quickly, leaving behind no trace of their amazing accomplishments.

*avalanche: a large amount of snow or rock sliding down a mountain

WORD FOCUS

Collocations for

chance

a **fair** chance
little chance
a **fifty-fifty** chance
ruin the chance(s)

WORD CHECK

Choose the correct words for the blanks from the highlighted words in the passage.

1. _____ to provide sb with the necessary things
2. _____ an organized journey with a specific goal
3. _____ another option
4. _____ a beneficial quality
5. _____ sb hired to help another person

1 **What is the passage mainly about?**
   a. how the Himalayan mountains are climbed
   b. the tall and beautiful peaks of the Alps
   c. an alternative form of mountain climbing
   d. the climbers who reached the top of Gasherbrum I

2 **Which is NOT true about alpine-style climbing according to the passage?**
   a. The name originated from the Alps of Europe.
   b. The climb starts from the bottom of the mountain.
   c. Climbers don't use fixed ropes or oxygen tanks.
   d. Porters carry the climbers' equipment and supplies.

3 **Messner and Habeler's attempt to climb Gasherbrum I was expected to be a failure because**
   _____.

   a. they hadn't climbed a mountain taller than 8,000 meters before
   b. no one had ever succeeded reaching the top of Gasherbrum I
   c. there was a high chance that they might encounter a snowstorm
   d. alpine style was thought suitable only for smaller mountains

4 **Why is alpine-style climbing better for the environment according to paragraph 5?**

   _____

5 **Use the words in the box to fill in the blanks.**

| equipment   reach   assistants   carry   accomplishment   garbage   alternative |

- Traditional way of climbing tall mountains
  - hire several _____, climb from camp to camp, bring a lot of _____ and supplies
- Alpine style of climbing
  - used by Messner and Habeler to climb Gasherbrum I in 1975
  - _____ everything yourself, climb to the top in one attempt
- Advantages of alpine style
  - less exposure to dangerous weather, not leaving behind _____

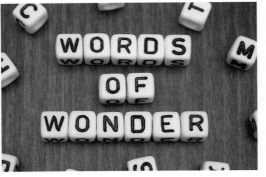

Puns create a double meaning by using words that either sound or look alike. They can also be made using words that have more than one meaning. Puns are often used to make people laugh, but they can make people think more deeply as well.

Puns using words with multiple meanings are known as homographic puns. A good example can be found in the following riddle: What is the difference between a conductor and a teacher? The answer is "A conductor minds a train, but a teacher trains a mind." In this case, two words each have two different meanings. "Mind," as a verb, can mean "to watch over." But as a noun, it means "brain." And the word "train" can refer to a mode of transportation or the act of teaching.

Homophonic puns, _____(A)_____, use two words that sound alike but have different meanings. For example, a sign in a pizza restaurant might read: Seven **days** without pizza makes one weak. Here, the pun is made with the word "weak," as it sounds the same as the word "week." Seven days do indeed make one week, while not eating pizza can make a person weak. Or at least that is what the restaurant owner wants you to believe.

But puns have also been used in some of the greatest literature in the English language. In *Romeo and Juliet*, for example, Shakespeare wrote, "Ask for me tomorrow, and you shall find me a grave man." This line is spoken by Mercutio after he has just been stabbed. While the word "grave" can mean "serious," here it also suggests that _____(B)_____ soon. This example clearly shows that puns, although they are often simply jokes, can also be used to make writing more powerful.

WORD FOCUS

◀ Collocations for

day

the **following** *day*
the **previous** *day*
the **very** *day*
the **other** *day*

WORD CHECK

Choose the correct words for the blanks from the highlighted words in the passage.

1. _____ a means of traveling from one place to another
2. _____ to protect and look after sb or sth
3. _____ to push a pointed object directly into sb or sth
4. _____ a series of words in a song, poem, or play
5. _____ a tricky, yet fun question that has a surprising answer

1 What is the best title for the passage?

    a. Tips for Being a Better Writer

    b. The Best Puns of All Time

    c. Puns: A Fun and Effective Way to Use Words

    d. Common Misunderstandings in English

DETAILS

2 What is the best expression for blank (A)?

    a. for example   b. as a result

    c. in addition   d. on the other hand

3 What is the best expression for blank (B)?

    a. he will feel sad   b. he will be dead

    c. he will act very serious   d. he will live underground

4 Write T if the statement is true or F if it's false.

    (1) Homographic puns use words that are spelled the same but have different meanings.   _____

    (2) Homophonic words may include "their," "there," and "they're."   _____

    (3) Using puns often makes writing less attractive.   _____

SUMMARY

5 Use the words in the box to fill in the blanks.

uses   double   powerful   simple   trains   laugh   sound

Pun

Definition
creating a _____ meaning with words that sound or look similar

Homographic
• uses words with more than one meaning
• example: "A conductor minds a train, but a teacher _____ a mind."

Homophonic
• uses words that _____ alike but differ in their meaning
• example: "Seven days without pizza makes one weak."

Uses
• makes people _____ and think deeply
• makes writing more _____

WARM-UP QUESTION • Do you know which countries use English as their first language?

More than 400 million people around the world are native English speakers. While all of these people speak English, distance and time have caused differences in the language. These can be anything from different accents to very different vocabularies.

Take the example of an American boy getting dressed in the morning. He puts on underwear, pants, a sweater, socks, and running shoes. A British boy putting on the same clothes wears underpants, trousers, a jumper, socks, and trainers. The American boy goes to high school; the British boy goes to secondary school.

The English spoken in Australia is also different. Australians use many words that English speakers from other countries may not recognize. They call a kangaroo a "roo," a chicken a "chook," and a farm a "station." When American or British friends meet, they say "Hi!" or "Hello!" But in Australia, the common greeting is "G'day!"

Of course, _____(A)_____, especially when you consider how many movies, books, and TV programs are shared between English-speaking countries. Thus, before a British book is published in America, editors change many words and spellings to help American readers understand it. But movies and TV programs are shown without changes, so it is sometimes hard for even native English speakers to understand them.

_____(B)_____, the various differences between British, American, and Australian English show the richness and variety of the English language. You will find it is fun to learn the unique words of each type of English. With a little practice, you will be able to guess a speaker's country from his or her accent and vocabulary. But be careful! If you make the wrong **guess**, you could make a British person "get angry," an American "get mad," or an Australian "go berko"!

WORD FOCUS

◀ Collocations for

guess

a **lucky** *guess*
a **wild** *guess*
a **rough** *guess*
make a *guess*

WORD CHECK

Choose the correct words for the blanks from the highlighted words in the passage.

1. _____ the state of including many different things
2. _____ to know sth because of previous experience with it
3. _____ to print copies of a book or magazine for public sale
4. _____ the space between two objects
5. _____ normal; occurring often

MAIN IDEA

1 **What is the passage mainly about?**
   a. diversity in the English language
   b. how to understand different styles of English
   c. the difficulties caused by the variety of English
   d. why English varies in different countries

DETAILS

 2 **What do Australians call a farm?**

_____

3 **What is the best expression for blank (A)?**
   a. we just ignore these differences
   b. these differences seem to be decreasing
   c. these differences can cause confusion
   d. we can do nothing about these differences

4 **What is the best word for blank (B)?**
   a. Therefore   b. Moreover   c. Nevertheless   d. Similarly

5 **Which of the following is NOT true according to the passage?**
   a. There are differences between American and British English.
   b. It is unlikely that native English speakers would misunderstand each other.
   c. Accent and vocabulary can help you to guess a speaker's country.
   d. To say they're getting angry, Australians use the phrase "go berko."

SUMMARY

6 Use the words in the box to fill in the blanks.

| unique | variety | meaning | confusing | recognize | share | native |

English may be the native language for over 400 million people worldwide, but over time and distance, it has developed a _____ of differences. This can make it hard for _____ speakers to understand each other. Though it is_____ at first, with a little practice you can _____ the patterns and more easily understand movies, books, and TV programs from all around the English-speaking world.

WORD REVIEW TEST

[1~4] **Choose the word that is closest in meaning to the underlined word.**

1. Max usually composes songs with a fast tempo.
    a. singing   b. speed   c. action   d. lyric

2. There is a fierce debate over how the money should be spent.
    a. honest   b. public   c. intense   d. continuing

3. She is a great pianist, but she is humble about her accomplishments.
    a. achievements   b. talents   c. interests   d. obstacles

4. The robber disappeared without a trace.
    a. trouble   b. arrest   c. harm   d. sign

[5~8] **Connect the matching words in columns A and B.**

A		B
5. reach •		• a. a snowstorm
6. be caught in •		• b. the mountain's top
7. play •		• c. the army
8. join •		• d. musical instruments

[9~12] **Choose the best word to complete each sentence. (Change the form if needed.)**

equip   flexibility   alternative   advantage   crime   ban

9. Singapore is a country with a low _____ rate.

10. Yoga improves your _____ and strengthens your muscles.

11. Contact lenses are a(n) _____ to eyeglasses.

12. This building is not _____ with fire extinguishers.

[13~16] **Choose the correct word for each definition.**

attempt   traditional   fixed   supply   participant   illegal

13. not allowed by law:

14. the act of trying to do something difficult:

15. someone who takes part in an activity or event:

16. securely fastened in a certain place:

[1~3] Choose the word that is closest in meaning to the underlined word.

1. His name was Roald, which is a <u>common</u> name in Norway.
   a. native   b. proper   c. female   d. popular

2. There are <u>various</u> reasons why people visit this city.
   a. a bit of   b. a variety of   c. a set of   d. a series of

3. Many people think the Internet is <u>indeed</u> a remarkable invention.
   a. really   b. simply   c. surprisingly   d. unexpectedly

[4~6] Connect the matching words in columns A and B.

A	B
4. cause •	• a. somebody
5. ask for •	• b. dressed
6. get •	• c. confusion

[7~10] Choose the best word to complete each sentence.

7. The little boy looked pale and _____.
   a. wrong   b. weak   c. powerful   d. alike

8. My best friend _____ her camera with me on our vacation.
   a. shared   b. recognized   c. helped   d. called

9. The politician _____ a book about his life.
   a. guessed   b. laughed   c. trained   d. published

10. *Robinson Crusoe* is a classic of English _____.
    a. riddle   b. program   c. language   d. literature

[11~14] Choose the correct word for each definition.

editor   consider   conductor   noun   verb   refer to

11. a word that describes an action:

12. to describe someone or something:

13. a person who decides what should be included in a book or movie:

14. someone who is in charge of a train:

Did you know that many of the **job**s you are familiar with today didn't actually exist until recently? For example, consider people whose work is related to smartphones. Until smartphones became popular in the mid-2000s, there were no "app developers" or "app marketers." Nowadays, however, thousands of people do these jobs. So what other kinds of jobs have appeared recently?

One of the most common new jobs is "data miner." Since modern market research relies heavily on customer data, companies are hiring experts to gather and analyze it. Those experts who look through large amounts of customer data to identify trends in _____(A)_____ are data miners. With their help, businesses can predict future trends or build personalized advertising.

Another recently created job is "drone operator." Drones have been around for a long time, but they were only used by the military or people who flew them as a hobby. Now, however, some big companies are making drones part of their business. Online shopping sites, for example, are planning to use them to make deliveries, and movie studios are already using them to film scenes from the air. All of these companies will require individuals skilled in flying high-tech drones.

Of course, new technology is not the only factor affecting job trends. Society's changing needs are also shaping the job market. For example, some companies are now hiring "sustainability experts" to help ensure that their business practices are environmentally sustainable. Other companies are even looking for "youth experts." These are mostly young people who can explain the behavior of the younger generation to older executives. Examples like these make it clear that job trends are changing rapidly. Can you imagine what kind of jobs will be available by the time you go out into society?

WORD FOCUS

🔗 Collocations for

job

a **temporary** *job*
get a *job*
lose a *job*
apply for a *job*

WORD CHECK

Choose the correct words for the blanks from the highlighted words in the passage.

1. _____ to make certain that sth occurs
2. _____ to begin to exist
3. _____ capable of continuing for a long time
4. _____ to read sth to find information
5. _____ being experienced or having good ability in a specific activity

MAIN IDEA

1 **What is the passage mainly about?**

a. jobs that are difficult to get

b. jobs that are popular today

c. changing job qualifications

d. jobs that have recently been created

DETAILS

2 **What is the best expression for blank (A)?**

a. job markets

b. consumer behavior

c. marketing campaigns

d. product developments

3 **Which of the following is a drone NOT likely to be used for?**

a. spying on enemy soldiers

b. filming a car chase for a movie

c. advertising online shopping sites

d. bringing purchases to consumers

4 **According to paragraph 4, what are the two factors that affect job trends?**

_____

SUMMARY

5 **Use the words in the box to fill in the blanks.**

| behavior   consumer   technology   collects   experts   delivers   environment |

Jobs That Have Evolved Recently

Data miner	Drone operator
(1) _____ and analyzes customer information for market research	(2) _____ items purchased online and films scenes by flying drones
Sustainability expert	Youth expert
ensures that companies don't harm the (3) _____ with their actions	explains youth (4) _____ to executives

19

Dale Chihuly is a glass artist from Seattle, Washington. One day while he was studying interior design at college, Chihuly saw some glassblowing. He was amazed by this skill

5 and decided to become a glass artist. Now his artwork is displayed in museums and public buildings worldwide, and people from many countries love his beautiful glass creations. I recently spoke with the artist at a coffee shop near his studio.

10 **Q:** _____ (A)

Chihuly: Glass is very beautiful because it shows light and color so well. I can shape it into many different forms. Also, glass is very fragile. It can break very easily, so it

15 seems very special. I create pieces of many different shapes and sizes out of brilliantly colored glass.

Q: _____ (B)

Chihuly: They come from the world around

20 me. My mother's beautiful flower garden inspires me. Also, I live near the ocean and I love to walk along the beach because the ocean gives me ideas. I also get ideas from other types of art, like Native American

25 baskets and blankets.

Q: Can you tell us about the glass ceiling you created for the Bellagio Hotel in Las Vegas?

Chihuly: I built the ceiling in the lobby of the Bellagio with the help of a hundred 30 other people. It is the largest piece I have ever made. It contains about one thousand multicolored glass flowers that hang from metal branches.

Q: _____ (C) 35

Chihuly: I work in the style of a movie director; I lead a team of glass artists at my studio. Each artist has a special job. We work together to create the pieces according to my designs. It's a wonderful 40 process.

WORD CHECK

Choose the correct words for the blanks from the highlighted words in the passage.

1. _____ to include sth
2. _____ very brightly
3. _____ to show specially arranged objects to people
4. _____ sth that a person has made (usually art)
5. _____ easy to break

MAIN IDEA

1 What is the interview mainly about?

a. the daily life of Dale Chihuly

b. the art world of Dale Chihuly

c. Dale Chihuly's most recent works

d. artists inspired by Dale Chihuly

DETAILS

2 Why did Dale Chihuly decide to become a glass artist?

_____

3 Match the questions to blanks (A), (B), and (C).

(1) (A) •   • ⓐ Do you usually create your art alone or with others?

(2) (B) •   • ⓑ Why did you choose to create art with glass?

(3) (C) •   • ⓒ Where do the ideas for your glass creations come from?

4 If something <u>inspires</u> you, it _____.

a. gives you new ideas

b. makes you feel calm

c. improves your health

d. helps you to concentrate

5 Which is true about Dale Chihuly according to the passage?

a. His works are displayed only in his studio.

b. He thinks that glass seems special because it is fragile.

c. His ideas for his artwork mainly come from his family.

d. He enjoys working by himself more than working with others.

SUMMARY

6 Match each topic to the correct paragraph in the passage.

(1) Paragraph 1 •   • ⓐ the largest work of art the artist ever created

(2) Paragraph 2 •   • ⓑ the qualities of glass that the artist admires

(3) Paragraph 3 •   • ⓒ a brief biography of the artist

(4) Paragraph 4 •   • ⓓ how the artist makes his works of art

(5) Paragraph 5 •   • ⓔ where the artist gets his inspiration

WARM-UP QUESTION • Do you enjoy a morning run?

At 5:30 a.m. in an empty parking lot, a group of people gather together for a morning run. But they are not jogging to lose **weight** or to train for a marathon. They are homeless people, and many of them are former drug and alcohol addicts trying to improve their lives.

They are part of an organization called Back on My Feet. Members go on group runs three times a week. The only requirement is that they must be clean and *sober for at least one month before joining the group. Besides having fun and getting exercise, members also get some useful benefits after 30 days. These include financial aid, housing assistance, and access to employment opportunities.

Back on My Feet started in 2007, when Anne Mahlum decided to organize a running club at a homeless shelter in Philadelphia. Many people told her that her idea would never work. "People said, 'These guys aren't going to want to run. They have other things to worry about,'" she explains. However, they were clearly wrong. In just six years, the club expanded to nearly 400 members in 10 different cities, and by 2019 it had spread to a total of 13 cities across the US.

The New York branch of Back on My Feet currently has about 60 members in its running club. In its first year, it helped 41 people find jobs, assisted 34 people in finding places to live, and enrolled 50 people in job-training programs. Morning runs may be the main activity for Back on My Feet's members, but they are just the first steps toward _____(A)_____.

*sober: having no drugs or alcohol in one's body

WORD
CHECK

Choose the correct words for the blanks from the highlighted words in the passage.

1. _____ sth that is necessary

2. _____ help given to sb in achieving sth

3. _____ a place that offers safety from danger

4. _____ sb who cannot stop doing sth

5. _____ one of many offices representing a large company

1 What is the passage mainly about?

    a. the most famous group run in the US

    b. Back on My Feet's job training programs

    c. an organization for helping the homeless improve their lives

    d. the US government's welfare system for the homeless

2 What benefits are given to Back on My Feet members 30 days after they join?

_____

3 According to paragraph 3, when Anne Mahlum started the running club, many people
_____.

    a. encouraged her

    b. were skeptical about the idea

    c. predicted it would attract public attention

    d. were worried about the health of the homeless

4 What is the best expression for blank (A)?

    a. getting a better job
    b. having a successful business

    c. winning a global title as a runner
    d. getting their lives back on track

5 Which of the following is NOT likely to be said by Back on My Feet members?

    a. I have to get up early in the morning three times a week.

    b. I used to be a drug addict but now I am making my life better.

    c. During the first month of group runs, it was hard to stop drinking alcohol.

    d. The organization helped me join a job training course.

6 Use the words in the box to fill in the blanks.

> shelters   running   branches   employment   homeless   benefits   enrolling

Back on My Feet is an organization that helps _____ people. It requires them to go on group runs several times a week. In return, they get help in acquiring financial assistance, housing, and _____. The organization was started in Philadelphia in 2007. It expanded to 400 members in just six years and now has _____ in 12 cities. The one in New York alone helped 50 people in its first year by _____ them in job-training programs.

"The world sends us garbage. We send back music." – Favio Chávez

The town of Cateura, Paraguay, was built on a landfill. Most of the population makes a living by collecting recyclable items from the trash that is brought daily to the town. In addition to poverty, another challenge the people of Cateura face is a lack of

5 education. Forty percent of the children there do not finish school. These children are often sent to work in the landfill.

In order to provide a better future for the children of Cateura, two men, Favio Chávez and Nicolás Gómez, wanted to _____(A)_____. However, instruments were too expensive. One day, Favio and Nicolás had an idea. The idea was to build their own

10 instruments out of materials found in the landfill, such as pieces of sheet metal, oil cans, rope, and broomsticks. That's how the "Recycled Orchestra of Cateura" was born.

The orchestra started with only a few musicians. But it has expanded to more than 35 members. It is now teaching more than 200 children how to play music and even how to build recycled instruments of their own. While the orchestra cannot immediately

15 fix problems like hunger and poverty, the education that it provides will lead to fewer children facing these problems in the future.

WORD FOCUS

⊜ Synonyms for

inspire

motivate
encourage
influence

Inspired by the Recycled Orchestra, people in other countries, such as Spain, Brazil, and Mexico, started their own recycled

20 orchestras. Not only has the Recycled Orchestra brought hope and a sense of pride to the residents of Cateura, but it has also shown that music truly has the power to change society.

WORD CHECK

Choose the correct words for the blanks from the highlighted words in the passage.

1. _____ a device that is played to make music
2. _____ at once; without delay
3. _____ a site where garbage is buried
4. _____ able to be remade into usable material
5. _____ the condition of not being able to afford basic necessities

1 What is the best title for the passage?

   a. An Orchestra That Brought Hope Through Music

   b. A Creative Plan to Fix the Economy of Paraguay

   c. The Controversy Surrounding the Recycled Orchestra

   d. Can Music Be the Answer to Global Poverty?

2 Which is NOT mentioned about the town of Cateura?

   a. where the town is located

   b. what most residents do for a living

   c. how much trash is brought there every day

   d. what difficulties the residents have

3 What is the best expression for blank (A)?

   a. organize a campaign for children's rights

   b. create a children's orchestra

   c. make a safe working environment for children

   d. set up a job training school in the town

4 What is the orchestra teaching to more than 200 children?

_____

5 Write T if the statement is true or F if it's false.

   (1) Many children in the town of Cateura drop out of school. _____

   (2) Favio and Nicolás made musical instruments using trash. _____

   (3) The Recycled Orchestra solved poverty in the town right away. _____

6 Complete the main idea of each paragraph using words in the passage.

   ▪ Paragraph 1: The people of Cateura face many challenges, including poverty and a lack of _____.

   ▪ Paragraph 2: Favio Chávez and Nicolás Gómez created a children's orchestra, which played instruments made out of trash from the town's _____.

   ▪ Paragraph 3: Children in the orchestra learn to play and _____ recycled instruments.

   ▪ Paragraph 4: The Recycled Orchestra has shown that music can _____ society.

WORD REVIEW TEST

[1~4] Choose the word that is closest in meaning to the underlined word.

1. He has displayed his artwork at a number of art galleries.
    a. painted   b. given   c. protected   d. exhibited

2. To lose weight, he tried not to eat foods that contain fat.
    a. include   b. taste   c. burn   d. gain

3. Rebecca was hired as the sales manager earlier this month.
    a. applied   b. promoted   c. employed   d. quit

4. They are taking every step to ensure that this kind of accident never happens again.
    a. warn   b. inform   c. take care   d. make sure

[5~8] Connect the matching words in columns A and B.

A	B
5. predict •	• a. the beach
6. fly •	• b. future trends
7. walk along •	• c. the artist
8. speak with •	• d. the drones

[9~12] Choose the best word to complete each sentence. (Change the form if needed.)

available   advertising   executive   creation   amazed   fragile

9.   Online _____ was used to promote her website.

10. Carl is a senior _____ of a multinational company.

11. Use some type of cushioning when you pack _____ items.

12. The audience was _____ by his performance.

[13~16] Choose the correct word for each definition.

expert   director   ceiling   film   individual   analyze

13. the top part of a room that connects the walls:

14. to examine something carefully in order to understand it:

15. the person who tells actors what to do:

16. to use a camera to record a story or shoot scenes:

[1~3] Choose the word that is closest in meaning to the underlined word.

1. These days I'm suffering from a headache due to <u>lack</u> of sleep.
   a. plenty   b. shortage   c. benefit   d. expense

2. I've <u>collected</u> information about the company I will apply for.
   a. created   b. compiled   c. organized   d. collaborated

3. The clothing store is <u>currently</u> having a huge sale.
   a. still   b. unusually   c. actually   d. now

[4~6] Connect the matching words in columns A and B.

A		B
4. go on	•	• a. the country
5. fix	•	• b. problems
6. spread across	•	• c. group runs

[7~10] Choose the best word to complete each sentence. (Change the form if needed.)

enroll   provide   inspire   expand   face   survive

7. Paul is planning to _____ his son in an English camp.

8. The purpose of the campaign is to _____ people to have a bigger dream.

9. The organization will _____ the unemployed with job-training opportunities.

10. The small office has _____ into an international enterprise.

[11~12] Choose the correct definition of the underlined word in each sentence.

> **work** *v.* **1.** to do a job to earn money: *He works as a photographer.* **2.** to put lots of time and effort in doing something: *Jina worked hard to get good grades.* **3.** to produce a desired result: *Our plan worked—they promised to support us.* **4.** if a machine works, it operates correctly: *My laptop doesn't work now.*

11. The pill didn't <u>work</u>. I still have a fever.   _____

12. The employees were forced to <u>work</u> long hours in the factory.   _____

WARM-UP QUESTION • Do you think rabbits can cause any harm to human?

Are rabbits dangerous? In most places, the answer is no. They are usually considered cute and lovable, and many people keep them as pets in their homes. But in Australia, rabbits are a big problem, due to the fact that they are a danger to the country's delicate ecosystem.

Rabbits were not indigenous to Australia. In 1859, however, a man brought 24 wild rabbits from England to Victoria, Australia, and released them into the woods so they could be hunted. Unfortunately, Australia is the perfect habitat for rabbits, as there are plenty of open spaces, lots of vegetation to eat, and few people. Also, Australian winters are **mild**, so the rabbits can breed all year. Most importantly, rabbits have fewer natural predators in Australia.

Soon there were millions of rabbits in Victoria. Most of the land in Australia isn't good for growing food, and the rabbits made this situation even worse. They ate so many plants that the soil underneath was eroded by the wind, leaving the land even less fertile. Moreover, some native animals which had to compete with the rabbits for food and habitat greatly decreased in number. Soon, the rabbits began to spread across the country. By the 1920s, the Australian rabbit population was estimated to be about 10 billion.

The Australian government has tried many things to control the rabbit population. At the beginning of the 20th century, they built long fences to keep the rabbits away from farmland. Contrary to the government's expectation, many rabbits crossed to the other side during construction, while others dug holes under the fences. The government also introduced diseases that kill rabbits. This significantly reduced the rabbit population, but only in certain areas.

Today, Australia's rabbit population is estimated to be about 200 million. Although the situation has improved, it is still a serious problem that the country is desperately trying to solve.

WORD FOCUS

⊜ Synonyms for

mild

gentle
temperate
warm
moderate

WORD CHECK

Choose the correct words for the blanks from the highlighted words in the passage.

1. _____ to have offspring
2. _____ plants and animals that live in a certain area by depending on each other
3. _____ able to support plant life, especially crops
4. _____ to wear away the surface over time especially by natural forces
5. _____ plant life in general, such as trees or flowers

1 What is the best title for the passage?

   a. Learning to Live with an Invasive Species

   b. Why There Are No More Rabbits in Australia

   c. Controlling Diseases Spread by Wild Animals

   d. Australia's Fight Against Unwelcome Guests

DETAILS

2 Write T if the statement is true or F if it's false.

   (1) Rabbits are native to Australia.

   (2) Australia's weather is good for rabbits to reproduce.   _____

   (3) Without rabbits, the land in Australia is perfect for agriculture.   _____

3 Why did some native animals in Australia greatly decrease in number?

   _____

4 Which is mentioned as Australia's effort to deal with the rabbit problem?

   a. planting poisonous plants that are harmful to rabbits

   b. increasing the number of predators that prey on rabbits

   c. spreading diseases that kill rabbits on purpose

   d. rewarding people who caught rabbits

5 Which CANNOT replace significantly in paragraph 4?

   a. considerably   b. greatly   c. accurately   d. substantially

SUMMARY

6 Use the words in the box to fill in the blanks.

bred   competed   control   fences   habitat   predators   decreased

Topic	how rabbits have become a threat to Australia
Background	▪ Some wild rabbits were brought to Australia from England in 1859. ▪ The rabbits _____ quickly across the country.
Problems	▪ The land became infertile. ▪ The population of some native animals _____.
Reaction	▪ Australia has tried to _____ the rabbit population. ▪ They built long _____ and introduced diseases that affect rabbits.

American Bison

The American bison is the largest land animal in North America. Males can weigh up to 2,000 pounds and stand 1.8 meters tall. Bison have huge heads, humps on their backs, and long, messy brownish-black fur. Bison travel together in herds looking for grass to eat.

Huge herds of bison once traveled across the grasslands of North America. They were
5 an important resource for Native Americans living on the plains. ■ They hunted bison and used almost every part of the animal. ■ They ate the meat and made tools and weapons out of the bones. ■ Blankets, clothing, and tents were all made from bison skins. ■ Bison calves are born in April, and the Native Americans believed that a kind spirit sent them bison each spring to help them survive.

10 All of this changed with the arrival of Europeans in the 1800s. The Native Americans only hunted bison when they needed resources. The Europeans, on the other hand, killed them in huge numbers for sport. They competed to see who could kill the most animals in one day. The effect on the environment was huge; when Columbus arrived in America, there were about 60 million bison. By 1890, less than 1,000 animals survived.

15 Bison were saved from extinction by the American Bison Society, which was formed in 1905. Many were raised in protected areas and then released into national parks. Today, there are about 500,000 animals. Although bison still need to be protected, they aren't at risk of extinction anymore.

Even though the bison can no longer live freely on the grasslands of North America,
20 it remains a symbol of the American Wild West. Each year, thousands of visitors to national parks can see herds of bison and imagine the past.

1 What is the primary purpose of this passage?

ⓐ to introduce ways to protect bison

ⓑ to criticize the Europeans for their behavior

ⓒ to describe the changes bison have gone through

ⓓ to warn people of the possibility of animal extinction

2 Look at the four squares [■] that indicate where the following sentence could be added to the passage.

Bison were also important to the Native Americans' spiritual beliefs.

Where would the sentence best fit?

3 All of the following are mentioned in the passage as possible uses of bison for Native Americans EXCEPT

  ⓐ food   ⓑ clothing   ⓒ equipment   ⓓ entertainment

4 According to the passage, the number of bison decreased because

  ⓐ the Europeans also started to hunt bison for food
  ⓑ diseases were spread when the Europeans arrived
  ⓒ many bison were killed by the Europeans for sport
  ⓓ the Europeans made profits by selling bison skins

5 The word extinction in the passage is closest in meaning to

  ⓐ dying out
  ⓑ getting lost
  ⓒ becoming old
  ⓓ suffering from a disease

6   Directions   Look at the sentence in bold. It is the first sentence of a short summary of the passage. Choose THREE answers to complete the summary. Wrong answer choices use minor ideas from the passage or use information that is not in the passage.

Large numbers of bison once lived in the American grasslands.

  ⓐ They have disappeared due to excessive hunting.
  ⓑ Native Americans hunted them with no consideration for their future.
  ⓒ They were an important resource in the lives of Native Americans.
  ⓓ Their population greatly decreased after the arrival of Europeans.
  ⓔ They became popular as a source of food among Europeans.
  ⓕ Thanks to protection efforts, they are now safe from extinction and live in national parks.

WARM-UP QUESTION • Have you read any Sherlock Holmes detective stories?

Most detective novels and stories share the same basic storyline: There is a **mystery** that must be solved by uncovering clues, questioning witnesses, and discovering the identity of the criminal. There are also a number of standard character types that occur again and again in detective fiction.

⁵ The heroes of these stories are almost always some sort of detective. The detective may be a professional or an amateur, but he or she must be very wise, observant, and logical. The detective uses these qualities to solve the crime along with the person who is reading the story.

These detectives often have a faithful assistant to help them out. This character is
¹⁰ sometimes referred to as a "Watson," after Sherlock Holmes's trusted companion. He or she is generally not as wise and logical as the detective and often makes foolish mistakes. However, the Watson character still manages to help the detective solve the crime.

Finally, all good detective stories must contain a villain. The storyline is usually focused on discovering who this person actually is. For this reason, in most cases, the
¹⁵ true identity of the villain isn't revealed until the end of the novel. Unlike the Watson character, the villain is usually _____ (A) _____. However, he or she always makes one big mistake and is captured in the end.

The next time you read a detective story, think about how these characters are described. But don't forget to try to solve the mystery, too! That's the best part of reading
²⁰ detective fiction!

WORD FOCUS

🔊 **Collocations for**

mystery

remain a *mystery*
be a *mystery* to sb
a **complete** *mystery*
an **unsolved** *mystery*

WORD CHECK

Choose the correct words for the blanks from the highlighted words in the passage.

1. _____ the plot of a story
2. _____ a main character in a story who is bad; the opposite of a hero
3. _____ one who observes criminal activity or an accident by chance
4. _____ a friend or partner who spends time with sb
5. _____ giving unending support for sb or sth

MAIN IDEA

1 **What is the best title for the passage?**

  a. Tips for Writing Detective Stories

  b. Characters You'll Meet in Detective Stories

  c. The Secret to Solving Fictional Mysteries

  d. Sherlock Holmes: Not as Smart as You Think

DETAILS

2 **Which is closest in meaning to <u>uncovering</u>?**

  a. finding b. providing c. hiding d. notifying

3 **Why is the true identity of the villain often revealed at the end of the story?**

  _____

4 **What is the best expression for blank (A)?**

  a. an outstanding fighter

  b. quick to solve crimes

  c. as intelligent as the detective

  d. described as a smart assistant

SUMMARY

5 **Use the words in the box to fill in the blanks.**

| solve   criminal   create   amateur   errors   described   identified |

Most detective stories include:

- Hero
  - can be a professional or _____ detective
  - is wise, observant, and logical
- Assistant
  - helps the hero _____ the mystery
  - makes silly _____
- Villain
  - is often not _____ until the end
  - is smart but makes a big mistake eventually

Kids enjoy fun and exciting stories, and reading helps their brains develop. But how can readers find the best children's books? One way is to look up the winners of major awards. There are many awards for children's literature. However, two of the biggest are the Newbery Medal and the Hans Christian Andersen Award.

The Newbery Medal has been given out annually since 1922. It was started by Frederic G. Melcher, a bookseller and editor. At that time, children's literature was often overlooked. Melcher hoped his award would bring public attention to children's books and make it easier for librarians to recommend good books to kids. He named the award after John Newbery, an 18th-century English publisher considered the "father of children's literature." Prize-winning works include *The Giver* by Lois Lowry and *A Single Shard* by Linda Sue Park.

The Hans Christian Andersen Award was started in 1956 to honor the famous writer's contribution to children's literature. It is given every other year to one author and one illustrator of children's books. Along with the quality of the work, the award's judges consider the ability of each nominee to see the world from a child's point of view and to stimulate children's imaginations. Some well-known past winners include Tove Jansson, the writer of the famous *Moomin* books, and Eiko Kadono, the author of *Kiki's Delivery Service*.

Although both of these awards are highly respected, there are some big differences between them. The Newbery Medal recognizes the best children's book of the year. The Andersen Award, on the other hand, isn't based on a single book. It celebrates the **lifelong** work of the people who receive it. Also, the Andersen Award considers writers and illustrators of all nationalities, while the Newbery Medal is only given to American citizens or residents.

WORD FOCUS

↔ Antonyms for

lifelong

temporary
transitory
momentary

WORD CHECK

Choose the correct words for the blanks from the highlighted words in the passage.

1. _____ to ignore or neglect the importance of sth
2. _____ to tell sb that sth is good and worth trying
3. _____ to make sth develop or become more active
4. _____ to publicly confirm sb's or sth's value of performance, as with an award
5. _____ time, effort, money, etc. given to sth to make it successful

1 What is the passage mainly about?

    a. the history of children's literature in the USA

    b. two awards that celebrate children's literature

    c. characteristics of the most popular children's books

    d. a children's book author who won many respected awards

DETAILS

2 Write T if the statement is true or F if it's false.

    (1) The Newbery Medal has been awarded every year since 1922.   _____

    (2) John Newbery was the creator of the Newbery Medal.   _____

3 What ability do writers and illustrators need to win the Andersen Award?

    _____

4 Which is closest in meaning to <u>residents</u>?

    a. occupations   b. landlords   c. inhabitants   d. novelists

5 Which of the following is NOT mentioned in the passage?

    a. who Frederic G. Melcher is

    b. when the Andersen Award was founded

    c. when Tove Jansson won the Andersen Award

    d. who are eligible for the Newbery Medal

SUMMARY

6 Use the words in the box to fill in the blanks.

| attention | named | illustrator | lifelong | nationalities | recognizes | quality |

Awards for Children's Literature

The Newbery Medal	The Hans Christian Andersen Award
▪ started in 1922 to draw people's ⁽¹⁾ _____ to children's books and to assist librarians	▪ started in 1956 to honor Hans Christian Andersen
▪ given to one author each year	▪ given to one author and one ⁽³⁾ _____ every two years
▪ ⁽²⁾ _____ the year's best children's book	▪ celebrates winners' ⁽⁴⁾ _____ achievements
▪ awarded to American citizens or residents	▪ awarded to people of all ⁽⁵⁾ _____
▪ includes Lois Lowry and Linda Sue Park as past winners	▪ includes Tove Jansson and Eiko Kadono as past winners

WORD REVIEW TEST

[1~4] Choose the word that is closest in meaning to the underlined word.

1. Experts gathered to restore this historically underlined important building.
   a. beneficial   b. significant   c. huge   d. national

2. Yellowstone National Park is a good habitat for wild animals.
   a. prey   b. home   c. herd   d. vegetation

3. I was raised by my grandparents until I was ten.
   a. put away   b. brought up   c. lifted up   d. cut off

4. The settlers were looking for a fertile land to grow crops.
   a. rich   b. local   c. native   d. vast

[5~8] Connect the matching words in columns A and B.

A		B
5. weigh •		• a. rivals
6. solve •		• b. 2,000 pounds
7. compete with •		• c. the grasslands
8. travel across •		• d. the problem

[9~12] Choose the best word to complete each sentence. (Change the form if needed.)

introduce   estimate   release   erode   hunt   save

9. Ron's annual income is _____ to be around $3 million.

10. The child was _____ from drowning by the lifeguards.

11. Thousands of balloons were _____ to the sky at the ceremony.

12. The cliffs on the shore have been _____ by the waves for decades.

[13~16] Choose the correct word for each definition.

delicate   resource   hump   spiritual   weapon   desperately

13. a round part that rises on an animal's back:

14. easily damaged and needing to be handled carefully:

15. something used to fight with or hurt someone:

16. something such as oil and trees that can be used by people:

[1~3] Choose the word that is closest in meaning to the underlined word.

1. He revealed his true self when money problems arose.

   a. showed   b. hid   c. suspected   d. kept

2. We should not overlook the importance of mental health.

   a. ignore   b. recommend   c. respect   d. celebrate

3. Authors spend much time reading other people's works as well.

   a. Illustrators   b. Authorities   c. Writers   d. Artists

[4~6] Connect the matching words in columns A and B.

A	B
4. enjoy •	• a. a witness
5. stimulate •	• b. fun stories
6. question •	• c. imaginations

[7~10] Choose the best word to complete each sentence.

7. The festival is held annually to _____ the war heroes.

   a. receive   b. honor   c. share   d. contain

8. Thank you for your _____ to success of our project.

   a. quality   b. fiction   c. nationality   d. contribution

9. The only _____ to the murder was a bracelet found at the scene.

   a. clue   b. assistant   c. villain   d. case

10. The scientist drew a _____ conclusion based on evidence.

    a. foolish   b. detective   c. faithful   d. logical

[11~14] Choose the correct word for each definition.

award   judge   identity   standard   resident   capture

11. who a person is:

12. to catch someone and keep him or her as a prisoner:

13. common and widely accepted:

14. a person who decides the winner of a competition:

These days, architecture is "going green," as more and more architects design buildings with efficiency and sustainability in mind. One great example is the Bullitt Center, a six-story office building in Seattle, Washington, USA. This impressive building produces more energy than it uses, and it is the new standard for sustainable
5 architecture.

The Bullitt Center was opened on Earth Day, April 22, in 2013. ⓐ Its primary purpose is to be a good model for office buildings pursuing sustainability. ⓑ The building has many eco-friendly **feature**s. ⓒ Also, solar panels on the roof provide all the building's energy. ⓓ For another thing, the elevator is located out of sight and the stairway offers
10 beautiful views of the city, which encourages people to take the stairs.

In summertime, blinds on the outside of the windows automatically adjust depending on the angle of the sun to manage the temperature inside the building. On cold winter days, a special heat pump system absorbs heat from deep in the ground. And then the system transfers this heat into the building, while triple-pane windows provide
15 fantastic insulation.

The roof of the Bullitt Center has holes that collect rainwater. This water is stored in an underground tank and is used throughout the building. Even though the building only uses about 500 gallons of water per day, the tank can hold up to 56,000 gallons! Finally, the Bullitt Center has a unique toilet system
20 that transforms human waste into fertilizer.

Thanks to these amazing features, the Bullitt Center will have its own steady supply of water and electricity—and will avoid utility bills—for the next 250 years! The building's creators hope that it will
25 inspire others to embrace green architecture and take practical action for sustainability.

WORD FOCUS

Synonyms for
feature

trait
quality
characteristic

WORD CHECK

Choose the correct words for the blanks from the highlighted words in the passage.

1. _____ more significant than anything else
2. _____ to change the position or setting of sth
3. _____ related to the sun
4. _____ a type of chemical that is added to soil to help plants grow
5. _____ a guideline or model that is accepted by people

READING SKILL

Understanding the flow
In smoothly flowing writing, all the sentences are arranged in the right order. No sentences stray from the topic. So, when reading the passage, see if individual sentences connect smoothly. Pay special attention to the connections between words and pronouns.

MAIN IDEA

1 **What is the best title for the passage?**

a. The Bullitt Center: A Green Model for the Future

b. The Dark Side of Green Architecture

c. New Emerging Technologies for Sustainability

d. Eco-Friendly Buildings Around the USA

DETAILS

2 **Which is NOT mentioned about the Bullitt Center?**

a. how many floors it has

b. where it is located

c. when its construction started

d. when it was opened

3 **Where would the following sentence best fit in paragraph 2?**

For example, there is a garage for bicycles but not for cars.

4 **How does the Bullitt Center manage the temperature inside the building in summer?**

_____

5 **Which is NOT true about the Bullitt Center's water system?**

a. The building collects rainwater through the holes in the roof.

b. The tank placed on the rooftop stores rainwater.

c. The amount of water the building uses a day is less than it can retain.

d. It will make the building's water supply self-sufficient for hundreds of years.

SUMMARY

6 **Use the words in the box to fill in the blanks.**

| insulation | elevator | fertilizer | adjusting | sustainable | rainwater | stairs |

Eco-Friendly Features of the Bullitt Center

- a garage for bikes, solar panels on the roof, and _____ encouraged for use
- Temperature maintenance
  - blinds automatically _____ in summer
  - a heat pump system storing solar heat
  - triple-pane windows providing _____ in winter
- Water and toilet system
  - _____ being collected through holes in the roof
  - human waste being transformed into _____

Reporter: Good afternoon, Dr. Kirkland. Recently, the world's honeybee population has been dropping dramatically. Strangely, nobody is sure why. Can you please explain the situation?

Dr. Kirkland: Certainly. Ever since the 1970s, the number of wild honeybees in North
5 America has been dropping rapidly. But now we're seeing a similar drop in the number of honeybees kept by beekeepers.

Reporter: I see. What are some possible causes?

Dr. Kirkland: The most likely cause is climate change. Bees depend on flowers, and the growing seasons of many plants are changing along with the climate. Scientists
10 are trying to find out what kind of effect this is having on honeybees. There are also some researchers who think that our cell phones are the problem. These phones use electromagnetic waves, which might be confusing the bees. If they can't find their way back to their hive, they'll most likely die. And finally, some scientists believe that toxic chemicals in some pesticides sprayed on plants are causing the honeybees to die.

15 **Reporter:** Interesting. But why should people care? Without honeybees, we'd have no honey. But surely there are bigger problems to worry about.

Dr. Kirkland: Honeybees are responsible for more than just honey. In fact, some experts believe that if bees were to go extinct, so would humans. This is because bees pollinate nearly 100 different crops, including soybeans, apples, and broccoli. It is estimated that one
20 third of our diet comes from plants that are pollinated by insects. Without honeybees, it is possible that we wouldn't be able to grow enough food to feed ourselves.

Reporter: I see. Clearly, this is a problem that should not be **ignore**d.
Thank you very much, Dr. Kirkland.

WORD FOCUS

⊜ Synonyms for

ignore

overlook
neglect
disregard

WORD CHECK

Choose the correct words for the blanks from the highlighted words in the passage.

1. _____ a structure that bees live in
2. _____ suddenly and in large amounts
3. _____ relating to both magnetism and electricity
4. _____ no longer existing as a species
5. _____ to help flowers reproduce by moving pollen

1 What is the interview mainly about?
   a. how honeybees pollinate crops
   b. the causes and effects of disappearing honeybees
   c. climate change caused by honeybee extinction
   d. influences the cell phone has on honeybees

DETAILS

2 Which is closest in meaning to likely?
   a. acceptable   b. probable   c. preferable   d. questionable

3 Which is NOT mentioned as a possible reason why honeybees are disappearing?
   a. abnormal changes in the climate
   b. interference caused by the use of cell phones
   c. poisonous chemical substances
   d. beekeepers' poor management of hives

4 According to Dr. Kirkland, what would we not be able to do without honeybees?

   _____

SUMMARY

5 Use the words in the box to fill in the blanks.

   | decreasing   pollinate   confuse   die   potential   extinct   toxic |

   An Interview with Dr. Kirkland
   ▪ The problem happening to honeybees
     - The number of honeybees is sharply _____.
   ▪ The _____ causes
     - The earth's changing weather is affecting bees.
     - Cell phones _____ bees and cause them to get lost.
     - _____ chemicals in some pesticides are killing off bees.
   ▪ The importance of honeybees
     - They _____ much of the food we eat.

Welcome to *My Blog*

HOME   CONTACT   BLOG

WARM-UP QUESTION • Do you like to drink tea?

For many British people, the morning must begin with a cup of tea. Otherwise, they can't make it through the rest of the day! It's no surprise, then, that the UK is one of the world's largest tea consumers. In this country, five cups a day is only average and for some this number is closer to 15 or 20. In fact, during World War II, Winston

5 *Churchill said tea was more important to British soldiers than weapons!*

The British tea habit started as a result of trade with China. In China, the tradition of drinking tea goes back to 3000 B.C., but it only arrived in the UK in the mid-17th century. The most common tea during these years was the green variety. However, in the 19th century, black teas became the preferred type. It was also around this time that

10 *a British tea culture started to form. British people developed a practice of drinking tea with milk and sugar, whereas in other countries people usually drank it plain. Tea was also consumed at specific times of day and during certain events. Terms like "tea break," "tea time," and "tea party," which are commonly used today, were created at this time.*

15 *British people also got really good at _____(A)_____. You can do this easily yourself. First, select a type of tea that you would like to try. Here are some popular choices: Darjeeling, Ceylon, English Breakfast, and Earl Grey. Place an infuser filled with loose tea into a teapot full of water. For*

20 *convenience, you can also use a teabag. Boil the water, and then let it sit for a few minutes. Your tea is now ready to serve, and you can add milk and sugar according to your taste!*

WORD CHECK

Choose the correct words for the blanks from the highlighted words in the passage.

1. _____ sth used to fight with or hurt sb
2. _____ sb who buys and uses things
3. _____ a type of sth
4. _____ the act of buying, selling, or exchanging goods
5. _____ a usual way of doing sth

READING SKILL

Inferring meaning
While reading, sometimes you have to guess meanings. To identify ideas that are not clear, you can use common sense or general knowledge. Also, you can guess meanings by using some hints from contexts or situations.

MAIN IDEA

1 What is the best title for the passage?

a. Various Types of Tea in the UK
b. The Tea-Loving Culture of the UK
c. The Most Popular Teas in the UK
d. An Increase in Tea Drinkers in the UK

DETAILS

 2 What can be inferred from the underlined part in paragraph 1?

a. Tea was more expensive than weapons.
b. British people really loved to drink tea.
c. Churchill was against using weapons.
d. The tea trade was more important than the war.

3 How did the tea habit start in the UK according to paragraph 2?

_____

4 Which is NOT true about the tea habit of the British in the 19th century?

a. They usually drank green tea.
b. They put milk and sugar in their tea.
c. They took breaks specifically to drink tea.
d. They enjoyed "tea time" and "tea party."

5 What is the best expression for blank (A)?

a. making a proper pot of tea
b. choosing a fine tea to taste
c. naming teas according to their tastes
d. matching each tea with the right kind of dessert

SUMMARY

6 Choose the proper topic of each paragraph.

(1) Paragraph 1	ⓐ the importance of tea in Britain
	ⓑ the history of tea use during WWII
(2) Paragraph 2	ⓐ how tea became part of British culture
	ⓑ similarities between British and Chinese tea cultures
(3) Paragraph 3	ⓐ the recipe for the most popular variety of British tea
	ⓑ instructions for preparing your own British-style tea

WARM-UP QUESTION • Do you know any festival for the dead in the world?

I n parts of Asia, the seventh month of the lunar calendar is known as the Ghost Month. It is said that every year on the first day of the Ghost Month, the gates of Hell open. This

5 allows ghosts to return to the world of the living and stay until the gates of Hell close again on the last day of the month. During this period, people remember their dead relatives and show respect to their ancestors.

The Ghost Month features three important days. On the first day, people burn small
10 items made of paper, representing clothes and money. This is believed to provide ghosts with these items in Hell. On the last day, people release paper lanterns onto rivers. These floating lanterns guide the ghosts to the items being **offer**ed to them.

The highlight of the month is the Hungry Ghost Festival celebrated on the fifteenth day of the month. During the festival, a delicious feast is offered to the hungry ghosts. In
15 return for the food, the ghosts bring good luck. According to one legend, a man named Mulian worried about his dead mother in Hell. She had to compete with other hungry ghosts for food. He traveled to Hell on lunar July 15 to give her food. Many people think this led to the tradition of offering food to the ghosts during the festival.

There are some taboos associated with the Ghost Month. People must not step on
20 paper items being burned as offerings. Wearing red or black clothing after 11 p.m. should also be avoided because these colors could attract hungry ghosts. Finally, people must not hang their clothes outside to dry, as passing ghosts may steal them.

In addition to honoring the dead, the Ghost Month gives people a lesson about
_____(A)_____. Worshiping ancestors encourages respect for family
25 members, while making offerings to ghosts represents the importance of sharing.

WORD FOCUS

≡ Synonyms for

offer

provide
give
present
grant

**WORD
CHECK**

Choose the correct words for the blanks from the highlighted words in the passage.

1. _____ to be a symbol of
2. _____ related to the moon
3. _____ sth that a society views as bad to do
4. _____ to try to get more than sb or do better than sb
5. _____ a plentiful meal that is held in celebration of a special event

1   What is the passage mainly about?

   a. different types of ghosts in traditional Asian legends
   b. a holiday during which people tell scary stories
   c. a celebration that brings the living and the dead together
   d. traditions that encourage family members to gather together

2   Write T if the statement is true or F if it's false.

   (1) People burn items during the Ghost Month in fear of ghosts' stealing them.   _____
   (2) People float paper lanterns on rivers on the last day of the month.   _____
   (3) The gates of Hell are closed on the Hungry Ghost Festival day.   _____

3   Why did Mulian worry about his dead mother in Hell?

   _____

4   Which is true about taboos associated with the Ghost Month?

   a. People must not burn paper items.
   b. People must not buy black clothes.
   c. People must not wear red clothes during daytime.
   d. People must not hang their laundry out to dry.

5   What is the best expression for blank (A)?

   a. religious rituals   b. proper behaviors
   c. preciousness of life   d. funeral arrangements

6   The sentence below is the first sentence of a short summary of the passage. Choose TWO
   additional sentences from below to complete the summary.

   During the Ghost Month, the gates of Hell are said to be opened.

   a. A man named Mulian started the Ghost Festival in honor of his dead mother.
   b. People traditionally burn paper items and serve delicious feasts for visiting ghosts.
   c. Red and black, the traditional colors of the Ghost Month, are worn by people.
   d. The activities of the Ghost Month not only honor the dead but also teach social
      lessons.
   e. Ghosts are trapped in Hell when their family don't make offerings to them.

WORD REVIEW TEST

[1~3] Choose the word that is closest in meaning to the underlined word.

1. The patient will be <u>transferred</u> to a bigger hospital.
    a. moved   b. treated   c. located   d. estimated

2. The artist <u>transformed</u> useless trash into a beautiful statue.
    a. stored   b. changed   c. embraced   d. buried

3. The situation was <u>clearly</u> worse than ever.
    a. extremely   b. uncertainly   c. strangely   d. obviously

[4~6] Connect the matching words in columns A and B.

A		B
4. pollinate •		• a. extinct
5. take •		• b. plants
6. go •		• c. the stairs

[7~10] Choose the best word to complete each sentence.

7. She was arrested for dumping _____ waste into the river.
    a. eco-friendly   b. similar   c. toxic   d. fantastic

8. Prices change according to _____ and demand.
    a. system   b. insulation   c. supply   d. utilities

9. _____ the things you really love and want.
    a. Pursue   b. Avoid   c. Inspire   d. Adjust

10. There can be some harmful _____ in our beauty products.
    a. crops   b. waves   c. fertilizers   d. chemicals

[11~14] Choose the correct word for each definition.

cause   automatic   efficiency   sustainable   confuse   population

11. the ability to make good results with minimal resources:

12. to disturb in mind or make it difficult for someone to understand:

13. the number of people or animals living in a particular area:

14. able to continue without harming the environment:

[1~4] **Choose the word that is closest in meaning to the underlined word.**

1. Americans <u>consume</u> 12 pounds of chocolate a year on average.
   a. serve   b. produce   c. import   d. eat

2. I had to <u>select</u> only one person among those people.
   a. choose   b. hire   c. meet   d. rescue

3. Children should learn <u>proper</u> table manners.
   a. complete   b. strict   c. appropriate   d. genuine

4. The teacher <u>guided</u> the students to their new classroom.
   a. caught   b. led   c. picked   d. offered

[5~8] **Connect the matching words in columns A and B.**

A		B
5. hang •		• a. a practice
6. boil •		• b. ready to serve
7. develop •		• c. clothes
8. be •		• d. water

[9~12] **Choose the best word to complete each sentence. (Change the form if needed.)**

dry   worship   weapon   represent   compete   encourage

9. The _____ displayed here were used during World War II.

10. The stars in American flag _____ each state of the country.

11. The players have been _____ for weeks to get medals.

12. This book will _____ your ambition to be an artist.

[13~16] **Choose the correct word for each definition.**

form   release   add   term   celebrate   attract

13. to show that an occasion is special by doing enjoyable activities:

14. to start to exist or develop:

15. a word or phrase used to mean something:

16. to make someone or something come:

Two players stare at each other in silence. Suddenly, one player makes a move. He captures the other player's king and wins the game! The game is chess, and it is centuries old. It is played on a checkered board, with squares arranged on an 8×8 grid.

You may have played chess before, but do you know where it comes from? The earliest version of chess appeared in India in the 6th century. According to a tale, a powerful king ordered a poor mathematician to invent an exciting game for him. The mathematician created a game with two armies, each led by a king. The game pieces included foot soldiers, horse riders, elephants, and *chariots, all standing on a board of 64 squares. The goal was to capture the **enemy**'s king.

The king loved the game and promised the mathematician a reward. The mathematician cleverly placed a grain of wheat on the first square of the board and asked the king to double it once for each of the other squares on the board. At first, the king thought it didn't seem like much. He ordered his servants to begin counting out the wheat grains. As the number of wheat grains continued to double, the pile of wheat became huge. Eventually, the king realized there wasn't enough grain in the whole kingdom. Laughing, he recognized that the mathematician was a _____(A)_____.

Over the centuries, the game became popular throughout India and started to spread west. Once in Europe, the game pieces began to develop into a European style. For example, instead of horse riders and chariots, there were knights and *rooks. By the 15th century, the game had started to resemble our modern version of chess. Although it was once a game for an Indian king, now it is played by people all over the world.

*chariot: a two-wheeled horse-drawn cart used in ancient battles
*rook: a chess piece that looks like a castle tower

WORD FOCUS

⊜ Synonyms for

enemy

rival
foe
opponent
competitor

WORD CHECK

Choose the correct words for the blanks from the highlighted words in the passage.

1. _____ with a pattern of squares of two separate colors
2. _____ a country or government led by a king or queen
3. _____ to have the similar appearance or qualities as sb or sth
4. _____ a grain grown and used to make flour
5. _____ a prize earned for doing sth well or as requested

1   What is the passage mainly about?
    a. the complex rules of chess
    b. the first board game in India
    c. how chess was created
    d. why chess became so popular

2   Why did the mathematician invent a new game according to paragraph 2?

    _____

3   According to the mathematician's request, how many wheat grains would there be on the
    fourth square on the board?
    a. 4   b. 8   c. 16   d. 64

4   What is the best word for blank (A)?
    a. liar   b. fool   c. magician   d. genius

5   Which is NOT true about chess according to the passage?
    a. A player must capture the enemy's king to win the game.
    b. It is played on a board with a checkered pattern of 64 squares.
    c. The original game pieces were related to the army.
    d. The original names of the game pieces are still widely used.

6   Use the words in the box to fill in the blanks.

    | servants   double   spread   invent   armies   led   reward |

    Chess is a centuries-old game played on a checkered 8×8 board. It was created when
    an Indian king ordered a mathematician to _____ a new game. The
    mathematician's game featured two _____ on a board of 64 squares. As a
    _____ he placed a grain of wheat on the board and asked the king to
    _____ it for each of the other squares. The king agreed, but there wasn't enough
    grain in the kingdom to fulfill the request. Over time, chess _____ to Europe
    and turned into the modern version that we know today.

WARM-UP QUESTION • Have you ever heard of Guy Fawkes Day?

If Guy Fawkes's plan had succeeded, we might remember him as the world's first famous terrorist. Instead, every year on November 5 people in Britain make models of him. Then, at night, they put the models on top of fires and burn them.

What did Guy Fawkes try to do? In 1605, James I was King of England. He treated Catholics very badly. Tired of the harsh treatment, Guy Fawkes and seven other Catholics made a plan to kill King James and every member of the English government. They hid a huge **bomb** under the Houses of Parliament. Guy Fawkes knew that King James and all the members of the government would be there on the night of November 5. But when he went to light the bomb, the king's guards found him and arrested him.

Immediately after his arrest, the English government declared November 5 to be a day of celebration. Over 400 years later, although the man himself is sometimes remembered in a more sympathetic way, "Guy Fawkes Day" is still celebrated. People spend several weeks getting ready for the big night. Stores start selling boxes of fireworks, and people buy their favorite kinds. Everyone collects wood, leaves, and garden trash to make bonfires.

Traditionally, children take their models of Guy Fawkes—called a "guy"—through the streets, shouting "A penny for the guy!" If people think it is a good model, they will give the children some money. The children then spend the money on fireworks.

On the night of November 5, people light fireworks in their gardens. Then they stand around the bonfire, cooking the traditional Guy Fawkes Day meal—sausages and potatoes. Finally, of course, they put the "guy" on top of the bonfire and burn him, thinking about _____(A)_____ .

WORD FOCUS

🔄 Collocations for

bomb

a **fake** bomb
drop a bomb
a bomb **threat**

WORD CHECK

Choose the correct words for the blanks from the highlighted words in the passage.

1. _____ to state sth officially or publicly
2. _____ unkind or cruel
3. _____ to take sb away for breaking a law
4. _____ having feelings of compassion for sb
5. _____ an object that explodes with colored lights and loud sounds

1   What is the best title for the passage?

a. The World's First Famous Terrorist

b. How Catholics Changed British History

c. The Fifth of November: Bonfire Night in Britain

d. The Unlucky Fate of a Great Hero

2   How did James I act toward Catholics?

_____

3   What is NOT likely to happen on Guy Fawkes Day according to the passage?

a. People enjoy their favorite kinds of fireworks.

b. People make a bonfire with wood, leaves, and trash.

c. Children sell models of Guy Fawkes on the street.

d. Sausages and potatoes are cooked at night.

4   What is the best expression for blank (A)?

a. the big mistake James I made

b. their anger at Guy Fawkes's failure

c. a traditional Catholic ritual

d. the crime that he tried to commit

5   Write T if the statement is true or F if it's false.

(1) Guy Fawkes's plan failed, and he was arrested.   _____

(2) Guy Fawkes was killed in a large fire.   _____

6   Use the words in the box to fill in the blanks.

| celebrate   bonfire   fireworks   failed   arrested   model   choose |

In Britain, every year on November 5 people _____ Guy Fawkes Day. The story
of Guy Fawkes dates back to 1605, when he tried to blow up Britain's Houses of
Parliament with a bomb to kill King James I and all the members of the government.
The plan _____, but people remember it each year by making a _____ of
Fawkes and burning it on top of a _____. They also light _____ and enjoy
a traditional meal of sausages and potatoes.

Australia is the land of the opal. This precious stone is the country's national emblem for a good **reason**: more than 90 percent of the world's opals come from a remote central area of Australia sometimes called the "Red Center." They are mined in severe climatic conditions in the desert areas of Queensland, South Australia, and New South Wales. Despite the abundance and popularity of opals, scientists were unable until recently to explain exactly how or why so many of the earth's opals formed in Australia.

Recent research findings at the University of Sydney have provided new insights into the mysterious formation of opals. Around 100 million years ago, an inland sea that covered 60 percent of Australia began to dry out. This caused extraordinary changes in the makeup of the rocks, soil, and minerals of the region. Acidity levels in the sea first increased and then decreased. This helped create ideal conditions for opals to form. Central Australia is known to be the only place on earth where these types of changes have ever occurred on such a large scale.

Surprisingly, these findings may help us _____(A)_____. The red-colored dirt and terrain of Central Australia share many characteristics with the surface of the Red Planet. In 2008, astronauts found opal-like deposits on the planet, strengthening the belief that opals may also exist there. The discovery of opals on Mars could be the key to further proving the similarities between Mars and the landscape of Central Australia. This means that scientists may be able to study biological processes possibly present on the faraway planet, right here on earth.

WORD FOCUS

◁ Collocations for

reason

a **main** *reason*
a **simple** *reason*
have (a) *reason*
give a *reason*

WORD CHECK

Choose the correct words for the blanks from the highlighted words in the passage.

1. _____ distant from a particular place or most places
2. _____ extreme; intense
3. _____ a naturally occurring layer of rock or other material
4. _____ new knowledge or understanding
5. _____ an object or design used as a symbol for sth

MAIN IDEA

1 **What is the best title for the passage?**
    a. Opals: Mysterious Hidden Gems
    b. Why Is Mars Called the Red Planet?
    c. Opals: A Link Between Australia and Mars
    d. How Gemstones Form in Desert Areas

DETAILS

2 **What is closest in meaning to <u>extraordinary</u>?**
    a. incredible   b. major   c. different   d. destructive

3 **How did acidity levels in an Australian sea change around 100 million years ago?**

_____

4 **What is the best expression for blank (A)?**
    a. preserve the opal-like materials on Mars
    b. better understand the environment on Mars
    c. save the natural resources of Central Australia
    d. copy the biological processes happening on Mars

5 **Which of the following is NOT true according to the passage?**
    a. Australia supplies the great majority of the world's opals.
    b. Most opals are found in the remote, desert areas.
    c. A moderate climate helped form Australian opals.
    d. Opal-like deposits were discovered on Mars.

SUMMARY

 6 **Choose the proper topic of each paragraph.**
    (1) Paragraph 1 •   • ⓐ the significance of possibly finding opals on Mars
    (2) Paragraph 2 •   • ⓑ introduction to Australian opals
    (3) Paragraph 3 •   • ⓒ the formation of opals in Central Australia

The San Andreas Fault

The San Andreas *Fault, the boundary between the Pacific *Plate and the North American Plate, runs along the northern coast of California and extends inland into the southern part of the state. It was discovered in 1895 and named after San Andreas Lake, which was formed by the movements of these plates.

5   These movements have helped shape the landscape of California in many other ways too. They have created beautiful mountains and valleys. But the San Andreas Fault is also a cause of much concern. The plates are still moving today, and they make the ground in the area dangerously unstable.

    The San Andreas Fault is a transform fault. This means that the plates that form 10 it are moving past each other. ■ Since they are moving in opposite directions, there is a high chance of serious earthquakes occurring. ■ This is especially worrisome because the fault runs through several highly populated areas. ■ Actually, a huge earthquake hit San Francisco in 1906. ■

    Earthquakes are very difficult to predict, but studying plate boundaries more carefully 15 may help scientists develop better warning systems for these natural disasters. The San Andreas Fault, one of rare plate boundaries on land, is much easier to study than other plate boundaries, which are mostly found beneath the ocean. Geologists are carefully studying it and watching for any signs that could help them predict when the next big earthquake may occur.

*fault: a large crack in the earth's crust
*plate: one of the layers of rock that form the surface of the earth

1   The word unstable in the passage is closest in meaning to

    ⓐ unhealthy

    ⓑ unnatural

    ⓒ unclear

    ⓓ unsteady

2 Look at the four squares [■] that indicate where the following sentence could be added to the passage.

It destroyed much of the city and showed just how destructive these plate movements can be.

Where would the sentence best fit?

3 In paragraph 3, the writer mentions San Francisco

    ⓐ to explain how a transform fault forms

    ⓑ to emphasize the danger of earthquakes

    ⓒ to give an example of an earthquake caused by the San Andreas Fault

    ⓓ to describe one of the most damaging earthquakes in recent years

4 According to paragraph 4, the San Andreas Fault is relatively easy for studying plate boundaries because

    ⓐ it runs along an urban area.

    ⓑ it has changed the entire landscape of the ocean.

    ⓒ it is not underwater unlike other plate boundaries.

    ⓓ its movements are easy to predict.

5 According to the passage, which is NOT true about the San Andreas Fault?

    ⓐ It extends through the state of California.

    ⓑ It was first identified in 1895 and named after a lake.

    ⓒ Underneath the fault, two plates are moving in the same direction.

    ⓓ It can provide a better understanding of earthquakes.

6   Directions   Look at the sentence in bold. It is the first sentence of a short summary of the passage. Choose THREE answers to complete the summary. Wrong answer choices use minor ideas from the passage or use information that is not in the passage.

The San Andreas Fault is a transform fault that runs through much of California.

    ⓐ Not much is known about its possible effects on this populated area.

    ⓑ The geological activity that it caused has now stopped.

    ⓒ It is located on the boundary between two major moving plates.

    ⓓ There is an increased chance of earthquakes in the areas around it.

    ⓔ Scientists are studying it to create better earthquake warning systems.

    ⓕ Although it has not caused any major earthquakes yet, it may soon.

WORD REVIEW TEST

[1~4] Choose the word that is closest in meaning to the underlined word.

1.   Mom asked me to separate the <u>trash</u> before disposing of it.
     a. bucket   b. equipment   c. garbage   d. luggage

2.   Jessica <u>invented</u> a device to help her sister walk.
     a. made   b. bought   c. installed   d. witnessed

3.   The police officer <u>ordered</u> them to step out of the car.
     a. threatened   b. shouted   c. persuaded   d. commanded

4.   A <u>huge</u> painting occupies a whole wall of my living room.
     a. large   b. old   c. wonderful   d. valuable

[5~7] Connect the matching words in columns A and B.

A		B
5. light •		• a. New Year's Day
6. cook •		• b. the traditional meal
7. celebrate •		• c. fireworks

[8~11] Choose the best word to complete each sentence.

8.   I found my bracelet under a _____ of books.
     a. board   b. pile   c. reward   d. version

9.   The police have _____ the person who started the fire.
     a. developed   b. succeeded   c. collected   d. arrested

10. Their goal is to _____ the number of customers who visit them.
     a. burn   b. include   c. double   d. appear

11. The president _____ May 1 a national holiday.
     a. declared   b. treated   c. hid   d. became

[12~14] Choose the correct word for each definition.

servant   arrange   burn   grain   modern   recognize

12. the seeds from certain plants, such as rice or wheat:

13. to place things in a particular position:

14. relating to or belonging to the present time:

[1~4] Choose the word that is closest in meaning to the underlined word.

1. It is hard to <u>predict</u> exactly where tornadoes will occur.
    a. warn   b. prove   c. investigate   d. forecast

2. There is an <u>abundance</u> of natural gas in the area.
    a. use   b. plenty   c. supply   d. import

3. An unexpected drought <u>occurred</u> in this region last year.
    a. repeated   b. continued   c. happened   d. stopped

4. They sent the child to be raised in a <u>faraway</u> country.
    a. distant   b. native   c. vast   d. strange

[5~7] Connect the matching words in columns A and B.

A	B
5. move in •	• a. a belief
6. strengthen •	• b. signs
7. watch for •	• c. opposite directions

[8~10] Choose the best word to complete each sentence.

8. There is growing _____ about violence of some mobile games.
    a. terrain   b. insight   c. popularity   d. concern

9. There were rich _____ of gold in this region until recently.
    a. deposits   b. minerals   c. directions   d. planets

10. The flights were delayed two hours due to _____ weather conditions.
    a. biological   b. remote   c. severe   d. mysterious

[11~14] Choose the correct word for each definition.

plate	precious	landscape	unstable	extend	mine

11. likely to move or change:

12. to dig resources out of the ground:

13. considered very valuable:

14. the whole visible part of a certain area:

WARM-UP QUESTION • If you could travel to another planet, which one would you choose?

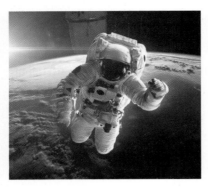

Most of us hope that space vacations will become possible in our lifetime. Imagine it for a moment. You hop into your personal spacecraft and <u>set off</u> for a hike on Mars or a star-gazing **trip** through the Milky Way. What should you take with you? Certainly, you'll need your camera and some tasty snacks for the journey. But above all, remember to wear the right kind of spacesuit. Without it, you won't survive on some of Earth's nearest destinations.

Let's start with Mercury. It is a fun planet to explore, with deep craters and high cliffs. However, Mercury has no air, so you definitely need a spacesuit with plenty of oxygen. Also, temperatures range from -173°C to 427°C, so wear a spacesuit that prevents you from freezing or burning.

Next is Venus. Frankly, Venus isn't a great vacation destination. It is too hot and cloudy, and its atmosphere is mostly carbon dioxide. In addition, the pressure of the atmosphere there is 90 times greater than it is on Earth. So, you need a *titanium spacesuit to protect you. Without one, you will be instantly crushed.

The safest destination is certainly our moon. Gravity on the moon is around 1/6th as strong as that of Earth. So you can easily bounce around and explore. Best of all, most spacesuits work well here. But make sure your spacesuit has temperature controls. On the moon, temperatures range from -173°C to 100°C. And you'll need oxygen, since there isn't any air there. But if you run into any problems, there should be a handy moon base nearby!

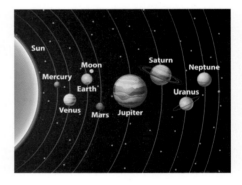

*titanium: a silver-white metal that is used as a strong building material

WORD FOCUS

⊜ Synonyms for

trip

journey
voyage
expedition
tour

WORD CHECK

Choose the correct words for the blanks from the highlighted words in the passage.

1. _____ a final location where sb or sth is headed
2. _____ a hole in the ground caused by an impact
3. _____ to be between two limits
4. _____ protective clothing that lets one survive in space
5. _____ to move in an upward and downward motion

1 What is the best title for the passage?

a. The Best Materials Used for Spacesuits

b. The Most Popular Space Destinations

c. The Latest Technology for Space Travel

d. The Right Spacesuit for a Space Vacation

2 Which is closest in meaning to set off?

a. prepare

b. carry out

c. depart

d. set up

3 How much pressure does the atmosphere on Venus have compared to that of Earth?

_____

4 Which of the following is true according to the passage?

a. The temperature range is greater on Mercury than on the moon.

b. Both Venus and the moon have no air, while Mercury has some.

c. Due to the hot and cloudy air, a titanium spacesuit is crucial on Venus.

d. The moon's gravity is stronger than Earth's gravity.

5 Use the words in the box to fill in the blanks.

freezing   extreme   atmosphere   gravity   explore   adjust   crushed

Proper Spacesuit for Destination

Mercury
- no air and _____ temperatures
- need a spacesuit with sufficient oxygen that prevents _____ and burning

Venus
- high-pressure of the _____ that is mostly carbon dioxide
- need a titanium spacesuit that can keep you from being _____

Moon
- the safest destination
- need a spacesuit that allows you to _____ its temperature

WARM-UP QUESTION • Have you ever thought about being an astronaut?

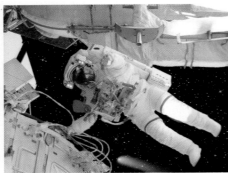

Y ou've probably seen pictures of astronauts in space. They are floating around and enjoying the feeling of weightlessness. But is living in space all fun and games? What is an astronaut's usual day like?

Actually, on the International Space Station there aren't any "days." The station speeds around Earth so quickly that the sun rises 15 times every 24 hours. However, astronauts must work and sleep on the natural 24-hour biological clock, or they would soon suffer from non-stop *jet lag. So the astronauts use an alarm clock to wake them up at the right time.

After waking up, it is time to get clean. Instead of taking a shower, however, astronauts give themselves a sponge **bath**. This is because, without gravity to pull it down, water clings to the body. It also conserves water, which is in limited supply on the station.

The astronauts then get dressed and sit down for breakfast. Space food is usually kept in plastic bags and drunk with straws. Otherwise, it will float around. Sometimes, the astronauts eat regular food, but it is fixed to the dish with straps, and the dishes, knives, and forks have magnets attached.

The astronauts have plenty of scientific work to keep them busy through the day, but they must also exercise. Human muscle and bone weaken in space, so there is an exercise bike to keep the astronauts fit. And what else must they do every day? Yes, what about the toilet? In space, toilets don't use water. A strong bar holds the astronauts onto the seat, and a fan empties the toilet like a vacuum cleaner.

At the end of their day, the astronauts are ready to fix their sleeping bags to a wall and get some sleep. Or they can find a window and enjoy the most popular pastime in space—watching the world go by hundreds of kilometers below.

*jet lag: tiredness you feel after taking a long flight because of the time difference

WORD FOCUS

◀ Collocations for

bath

take a *bath*
a **warm** *bath*
bath **water**
bath **time**

WORD CHECK

Choose the correct words for the blanks from the highlighted words in the passage.

1. _____ normal, typical
2. _____ to protect sth from being used up
3. _____ a narrow piece of material like leather or cloth used to hold or tie sth
4. _____ to have pain or discomfort from sth
5. _____ a hobby or sth you enjoy doing when you are not working

READING SKILL

Inferring meaning

To identify ideas that are not directly stated in writing, we can make use of common sense or our knowledge of the world. Also, we can guess meanings by using some clues from context or situations.

MAIN IDEA

1 **What is the passage mainly about?**

a. training to be an astronaut

b. purposes of space research

c. a typical day for astronauts

d. difficulties astronauts go through

DETAILS

 2 **It can be inferred from paragraph 4 that usual space food must be _____.**

a. fresh

b. healthy

c. delicious

d. processed

3 **Why do astronauts have to exercise in space?**

_____

4 **Which is NOT true about astronauts according to the passage?**

a. They need an alarm clock to maintain their biological rhythms.

b. They have sponge baths instead of regular showers.

c. They fix their sleeping bags to a wall to get some sleep.

d. One of their important duties is to watch Earth before going to sleep.

SUMMARY

5 **Use the words in the box to fill in the blanks.**

| strapped | bar | floats | weakens | conserved | clock | straw |

A Day in Space

Getting clean	Eating
▪ Astronauts take sponge baths. ▪ Water must be (1)_____.	▪ Food is usually eaten from a plastic bag with a (2)_____. ▪ Regular food must be (3)_____ to the plates.
Exercising	**Using the toilet**
▪ Living in space (4)_____ muscles and bones. ▪ They ride exercise bikes.	▪ No water is used. ▪ A (5)_____ keeps them on the seat.

WARM-UP QUESTION
• Do you know how car safety tests are carried out?

Decades ago, people rarely survived serious car accidents. Cars today are much safer, thanks to improvements in safety tests. During a car safety test, a new car is crashed into a wall at high **speed**. Inside the car there are passenger-sized dolls called "crash test dummies." By studying these crash test dummies, scientists can see _____(A)_____ in a crash and improve the safety of the car.

Today's crash test dummies are built to be as much like human beings as possible. They have ribs like ours inside their artificial skin. They even have backbones made out of metal and rubber. Their knees and ankles are designed to act just like ours do in accidents. They also come in different sizes; there is an entire dummy family, including smaller "female" and even smaller "child" dummies.

The dummies have three different kinds of sensors that measure the impact of a crash. Sensors in the head, legs, and other areas show how fast a body part moves during a crash. Another sensor can record how much pressure our bones can take before breaking. Finally, a sensor in the chest area shows whether a crash would cause injuries that could lead to death.

Crash test dummies are very high-tech, but they're also extremely expensive. Each one costs more than $100,000. A cheaper alternative, however, is being developed. "Virtual" crash test dummies exist only on the computer screen, yet it may be possible to make them even more lifelike than today's crash test dummies. They can easily be altered to resemble people of any height or weight, and, best of all, they can be used over and over without being damaged. In the future, they may completely change the way crash tests are conducted.

WORD FOCUS

Collocations for

speed

an **average** *speed*
at **full** *speed*
reduce the *speed*
speed **limit**

WORD CHECK

Choose the correct words for the blanks from the highlighted words in the passage.

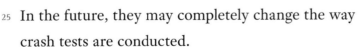

1. _____ to find the size, length, or amount of sth
2. _____ appearing to be alive
3. _____ to come into contact with sth very hard
4. _____ to make slight changes to sth
5. _____ equipment that can feel or sense sound, light, motion, etc.

1 **What is the passage mainly about?**

    a. how to survive serious car accidents

    b. the lifelike dolls used for car crash tests

    c. various kinds of high-tech car safety tests

    d. the sensor technology adopted for the safety of drivers

2 **What is the best expression for blank (A)?**

    a. how the engine in a car reacts

    b. what kind of cars are damaged the most

    c. what would happen to real passengers

    d. where passengers are most likely to be

3 **Which is closest in meaning to artificial?**

    a. natural   b. beautiful

    c. sensitive   d. man-made

4 **What does a sensor in dummies' chest area do according to the passage?**

_____

5 **Which is NOT true about crash test dummies according to the passage?**

    a. They are produced in various sizes.

    b. They have ribs and backbones like humans.

    c. Each of their sensors costs more than $100,000.

    d. Virtual crash test dummies can be reused.

6 **Match each topic to the correct paragraph in the passage.**

    (1) Paragraph 1 •   • ⓐ improvements in car safety through crash tests

    (2) Paragraph 2 •   • ⓑ the development of virtual dummies

    (3) Paragraph 3 •   • ⓒ purposes of sensors placed in dummies

    (4) Paragraph 4 •   • ⓓ the human-like bodies of crash test dummies

The Eiffel Tower in Paris is one of the most famous structures ever created by humans. But not many people know the inspiration behind the design of the tower. As a matter of fact, the Eiffel Tower is modeled on a human thigh bone!

Interesting discoveries were made about the thigh bone in the 1850s. Anatomists were studying the top of the thigh bone, called the head, which connects to the hip joint. The thigh bone head is specially designed to bear the weight of a standing human being. Its internal structure is made up of many small interconnected *struts like the bars of a cage. This interesting structure is what enables the thigh bone to support the body's weight. The engineer Gustave Eiffel was very impressed with the structure of the thigh bone, and he used it to design the Eiffel Tower. This structure is why the tower can remain **steady** in strong winds.

Besides the Eiffel Tower, other human-made structures modeled on nature can be seen in many places in the world. For example, the roof of Munich's Olympic Stadium is based on the design of a dragonfly's wings. It is made up of thousands of tiny transparent sections, giving it strength but also allowing light to pass through. And gecko tape, which is stronger than glue but easily sticks on and peels off, was developed based on the microscopic hairs on a gecko lizard's toes.

These and other innovations show we actually have much to _____(A)_____. People are beginning to realize that solutions to many of the problems we face may exist in the natural world already. All we have to do is find them.

*strut: a supporting bar in a structure

**WORD
CHECK**

Choose the correct words for the blanks from the highlighted words in the passage.

1. _____ able to be seen through
2. _____ a sticky substance that is used to join things together
3. _____ the upper part of the leg
4. _____ to plan or shape sth based on sth else
5. _____ a new idea or method which has been introduced

1 What is the passage mainly about?

   a. the creative ability of humans

   b. great structures in the natural world

   c. innovations following principles of nature

   d. protecting nature with modern inventions

2 What is the thigh bone head designed to do?

_____

3 Match each object with the inspiration for its design.

   (1) the Eiffel Tower   •   • ⓐ dragonfly's wings

   (2) Munich's Olympic Stadium •   • ⓑ hairs on a lizard's toes

   (3) gecko tape   •   • ⓒ top of the thigh bone

4 What is the best expression for blank (A)?

   a. do to protect our planet   b. explain to our children

   c. learn from nature   d. gain by designing buildings

5 Which of the following is NOT true according to the passage?

   a. The human thigh bone is connected to the hip joint.

   b. Gustave Eiffel was an anatomist who designed the Eiffel Tower.

   c. The Eiffel Tower can stand strong winds due to its structure.

   d. Light can pass through the roof of Munich's Olympic Stadium.

6 Use the words in the box to fill in the blanks.

solutions   inspired   design   exist   modeled   changes   bear

The _____ of the Eiffel Tower is based on that of a human thigh bone. Thanks to this borrowed structure, the tower can _____ strong winds. There are many other examples of how nature has _____ humans. The roof of a stadium was _____ on dragonfly wings, and gecko tape was based on a lizard's toes. These examples suggest that nature has _____ to human problems, and we can learn from it.

WORD REVIEW TEST

[1~4] Choose the word that is closest in meaning to the underlined word.

1. She tries to keep herself physically <u>fit</u> by exercising every day.
    a. young   b. healthy   c. tiny   d. weak

2. We turn off all the lights after ten o'clock in order to <u>conserve</u> energy.
    a. develop   b. produce   c. fix   d. save

3. His new movie is <u>definitely</u> worth watching.
    a. never   b. readily   c. surprisingly   d. certainly

4. My hair <u>clings to</u> my forehead when I sweat.
    a. calls to   b. looks after   c. sticks to   d. leans on

[5~7] Connect the matching words in columns A and B.

A	B
5. set off for •	• a. a journey
6. hop into •	• b. a spacesuit
7. wear •	• c. a spacecraft

[8~11] Choose the best word to complete each sentence. (Change the form if needed.)

survive   float   weaken   attach   burn   instantly

8.   White clouds are _____ in the sky.

9.   There is a price tag _____ to everything.

10. Your bones can _____ if you drink too much Coke.

11. Emma knew _____ that her son was lost in the crowded store.

[12~15] Choose the correct word for each definition.

gravity   handy   magnet   explore   crush   atmosphere

12. the gases that surround the surface of a planet:

13. to use force to break something:

14. the force that pulls objects toward the center of a planet:

15. a special piece of metal that attracts other metal objects toward it:

[1~4] Choose the word that is closest in meaning to the underlined word.

1.   Thanks to your call, I wasn't late for the meeting.
     a. In spite of   b. Because of   c. In favor of   d. According to

2.   Staying in the sun too long can lead to a headache.
     a. result in   b. stop from   c. deal with   d. belong to

3.   A few technological innovations have changed our lives completely.
     a. chances   b. solutions   c. directions   d. developments

4.   We've taken a different path that will enable us to get there faster.
     a. force   b. allow   c. require   d. prevent

[5~7] Connect the matching words in columns A and B.

A	B
5. make •	• a. steady
6. support •	• b. a discovery
7. remain •	• c. the body's weight

[8~11] Choose the best word to complete each sentence. (Change the form if needed.)

resemble   injury   impact   model   conduct   measure

8.   You don't _____ your father at all.

9.   It's very difficult to _____ the damage caused by the accident.

10. The educational system of the country is _____ on the American one.

11. The _____ of the earthquake was greater than expected.

[12~15] Choose the correct word for each definition.

passenger   virtual   inspiration   joint   anatomist   pressure

12. seeming to be real, but not actually existing:

13. a person who travels in a vehicle:

14. a part of your body that can bend:

15. a force pushing on someone or something:

WARM-UP QUESTION • Do you agree that negative thoughts can lead to bad results?

The placebo **effect** is a well-known phenomenon. Patients can receive positive effects from fake medicine due to their expectation that it will help them. But this can also work in the opposite way. Although it is less commonly discussed, this situation is called the nocebo effect.

5 According to numerous studies, a significant number of patients stop taking the fake medicine given to them because of unpleasant side effects. For example, when testing a drug for a chronic pain disorder, researchers gave some of the subjects fake medicine. They found that 11% of these people quit the study because of dizziness and nausea. Those subjects expected these side effects to occur, so they truly felt as though 10 they were suffering from them.

The nocebo effect can also occur when patients take real medication. When doctors tell their patients about the possible side effects of a medication, the patients are more likely to experience them. Even the specific words that a doctor uses can cause the nocebo effect. For example, women giving birth often receive a shot to reduce their pain. In an 15 experiment, some women were told that the shot would help them feel better. The others were told that the shot itself would hurt. Due to the doctor's word choice, the latter group reported the shot to be more _____(A)_____ than the former group did.

Because of the nocebo effect, doctors face a difficult decision. On one hand, they want to be completely honest with their patients. But, on the other hand, they don't 20 want to cause their patients to experience unnecessary pain or side effects. Experts believe that the best solution is for doctors to _____(B)_____ clearly with their patients, but to avoid emphasizing negative things.

WORD CHECK

Choose the correct words for the blanks from the highlighted words in the passage.

1. _____ not real
2. _____ sb or sth used in a scientific experiment
3. _____ sth that happens naturally in nature or society
4. _____ many; great in number
5. _____ a condition of the mind or body that is not normal or healthy

Understanding the details

Details give readers a better explanation of what the author is trying to say. Details can be used to further describe the topic or to give examples. When dealing with detail questions, only use the information given in the text. Do not infer!

MAIN IDEA

1 What is the passage mainly about?

    a. a problem caused by taking fake medicine

    b. a study that proves the placebo effect is not real

    c. a new kind of medicine without any side effects

    d. a psychological effect caused by negative expectations

DETAILS

2 Why did 11% of subjects quit the study about a drug for a chronic pain disorder?

_____

3 What is the best pair for blanks (A) and (B)?

	(A)	(B)
a.	terrible	agree
b.	painful	communicate
c.	enjoyable	interact
d.	dangerous	interfere

4 Write T if the statement is true or F if it's false.

    (1) The nocebo effect is related to reducing chronic pain. _____

    (2) The nocebo effect can be observed when a patient takes either fake or real medicine. _____

    (3) A doctor's word choice could affect the degree of pain a patient feels. _____

SUMMARY

5 Use the words in the box to fill in the blanks.

possible   opposite   suffering   dishonest   expectations   experiments   choice

The Nocebo Effect

The _____ of the placebo effect
▪ Patients experience negative side effects due to their _____.

Ways it can occur
▪ Patients are given fake medicine.
▪ Patients are given real medicine and told about _____ side effects.

Doctors' dilemma
▪ They don't want to be _____ with patients.
▪ They don't want to cause unnecessary discomfort.

WARM-UP QUESTION • What do you usually do when you catch a cold?

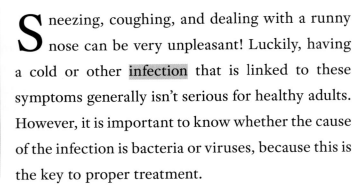

Sneezing, coughing, and dealing with a runny nose can be very unpleasant! Luckily, having a cold or other infection that is linked to these symptoms generally isn't serious for healthy adults.

5 However, it is important to know whether the cause of the infection is bacteria or viruses, because this is the key to proper treatment.

Bacteria are responsible for some infections, such as those of the ears, lungs, *airways, and throat. However, most respiratory infections, including the **common**
10 cold and flu, are caused by viruses. Bacteria and viruses are very different. Bacteria are one-celled organisms that divide in order to multiply. Meanwhile, viruses are much smaller and cannot survive or multiply on their own. They spread by taking over cells and using them to reproduce.

One of the most important differences between bacteria and viruses is how they
15 are treated. Once doctors do tests to find the cause of an infection, they can figure out which kind of medicine to give to their patients. Antibiotics kill bacteria but do not fight viruses. A different type of medicine is needed to stop a virus from taking over cells and reproducing. Giving antibiotics to patients when they are not necessary can be dangerous. This is because the more bacteria are exposed to antibiotics, the more they are able to
20 adapt and build up a resistance to them. When antibiotics stop working against certain bacteria, it becomes much harder to treat infections caused by them.

Of course, it is best to try not to get respiratory infections in the first place. Viruses in particular are easily spread because they can survive in the air for some time after someone sneezes or coughs. They can also be spread to shared objects, such as doorknobs.
25 That's why regular hand washing is so important.

*airway: the passage that carries air from the nose or mouth into the lungs

WORD FOCUS

↔ Antonyms for

common

rare
unusual
exceptional

WORD
CHECK

Choose the correct words for the blanks from the highlighted words in the passage.

1. _____ the ability not to be affected by sth
2. _____ related to the body's system of breathing
3. _____ an illness caused by bacteria or viruses
4. _____ to modify ideas or behavior to deal with a new circumstance
5. _____ to create copies of oneself

1 What is the passage mainly about?

   a. difficulties related to respiratory infections

   b. the overuse of antibiotics in humans

   c. differences between bacteria and viruses

   d. how an infection can become a serious medical problem

2 According to paragraph 1, why is it important to know whether the cause of the infection is bacteria or viruses?

   _____

3 Write T if the statement is true or F if it's false.

   (1) Viruses account for most respiratory infections.   _____

   (2) Bacteria can reproduce by themselves.   _____

   (3) Antibiotic drugs are effective against viruses.   _____

4 Which of the following is NOT mentioned in the passage?

   a. which body parts bacteria cause infections in

   b. which tests doctors do to find the cause of an infection

   c. why the careful use of antibiotics is important

   d. how viruses move from one person to another

5 Use the words in the box to fill in the blanks.

bigger	regularly	causes	symptoms	kill	multiply	smaller

- _____ of respiratory infections
  - Bacteria and viruses are responsible for respiratory infections.
- Differences between bacteria and viruses
  - Bacteria are _____ organisms than viruses.
  - Only bacteria can survive and _____ on their own.
  - Antibiotics _____ bacteria, but not viruses.
- Prevention methods
  - Wash your hands _____ to avoid catching viruses.

Have you ever felt like you know the answer to a question, but for some reason you just can't think of the right word? This state is known as "*lethologica," or the "tip of the tongue" phenomenon. One of the most common signs of lethologica is partial memory. For example, one might know that a word begins with a certain letter, or they might even be convinced of the number of syllables it has, but they can't remember the rest. Sometimes, similar-sounding words come to mind.

There are several theories as to why lethologica occurs. The first theory says that lethologica occurs when the target word is not completely activated in one's memory. This could happen when not all the cues normally used to trigger the target word in one's mind are present. Another theory suggests that memories of similar-sounding words block the memory of the word one is trying to remember. The last theory claims that lethologica happens when the memory of a word's sound becomes disconnected from that of its meaning in the mind.

Researchers' opinions are divided when it comes to the effect of lethologica on memory. Some believe that struggling but then retrieving a memory strengthens one's ability to recall it, while others think that this process makes it more likely for lethologica to happen again.

While it might be annoying to have a word on the tip of your tongue, you don't need to worry even if it happens to you. It is a natural phenomenon, and researchers have **discover**ed that it is common for speakers of different languages all over the world. It doesn't mean there is a problem with your brain or your memory, so don't let lethologica stress you out!

*lethologica: a phenomenon in which one is unable to retrieve a particular word from memory

WORD FOCUS

= Synonyms for

discover

find out
learn
realize

WORD CHECK

Choose the correct words for the blanks from the highlighted words in the passage.

1. _____ not whole
2. _____ to bring a memory to one's mind
3. _____ a situation or condition that sb or sth is in
4. _____ a sound with a single vowel, which forms a word or part of a word
5. _____ to cause a machine, function, or process to start

1 What is the best title for the passage?

   a. Lethologica: Annoying, but Natural
   b. How to Overcome the "Tip of the Tongue"
   c. Lethologica: A Rare Sign of Mental Decline
   d. How the Brain Stores New Words in Memory

2 Who is likely to be experiencing lethologica? [Choose two.]

> Jesse: I can't recall the answer. But I am sure it has five syllables.
> Alice: I think I am good at writing, but poor at speaking.
> Claire: The band's name starts with a *D*, but I can't remember the exact name.
> Phil: My memory was good when I was younger, but it is failing now.

   a. Jesse   b. Alice   c. Claire   d. Phil

3 According to the theories, lethologica can happen when _____.

   a. the memory of a target word blocks that of a similar-sounding word
   b. our brain gets too much stress while recalling a word
   c. the cues needed to recollect the target word are fully activated
   d. the memory of a word's sound is cut off from its meaning

4 What does this process refer to in paragraph 3?

   _____

5 Which is NOT true about lethologica?

   a. It is another name for the "tip of the tongue" phenomenon.
   b. Its effect on memory is disputable.
   c. Speakers of many different languages experience it.
   d. It is a signal of a decline in our memory.

6 Match each topic to the correct paragraph in the passage.

   (1) Paragraph 1 •   • ⓐ possible reasons why lethologica occurs
   (2) Paragraph 2 •   • ⓑ researchers' opinions on the effect of lethologica
   (3) Paragraph 3 •   • ⓒ why lethologica is a natural phenomenon
   (4) Paragraph 4 •   • ⓓ meaning and examples of lethologica

Have you ever been surprised to see negative reviews of a movie that you enjoyed? This surprise can be explained by the false consensus effect. It is the assumption that most other people have the same opinions we do.

Many experiments have proven that the false consensus effect is real. In one study, researchers asked subjects if they would agree to walk around the campus for thirty minutes while wearing a *sandwich board with an advertisement. The subjects were also asked to estimate how many people would agree or **refuse** to carry the board. On average, both those who agreed to carry the board and those who refused estimated that the majority of others would make the same choice they did.

There are three main causes of the false consensus effect. First, we predict how others think generally based on opinions of our friends and family, whose beliefs are likely to be similar to ours. Second, believing that other people think like we do makes us feel good about ourselves. Finally, we are more likely to notice and pay attention to other people's opinions when they are the same as ours.

The false consensus effect becomes stronger when it comes to beliefs that we hold firmly. For example, if you are absolutely convinced that a certain law will help reduce crime in your neighborhood, then you will be highly likely to believe that most others in your neighborhood will also support the law.

Do you think the false consensus effect is real? Or do you doubt it? You might think that others have the same opinion as you. If so, you might be experiencing the false consensus effect right now! Therefore, try to remember that _____(A)_____, even when it seems like common sense!

*sandwich board: a pair of connected boards that are hung over someone's shoulders for the purpose of advertising

WORD FOCUS

⟷ Antonyms for

refuse

accept
agree
consent

WORD CHECK

Choose the correct words for the blanks from the highlighted words in the passage.

1. _____ more than half of a group
2. _____ to express agreement with an idea, law, or system
3. _____ basic way of thinking that society expects everyone to have
4. _____ to become aware of
5. _____ to judge the value, size, or amount of sth approximately

1 What is the passage mainly about?

   a. how we can counteract the false consensus effect

   b. why our intuitions often turn out to be correct

   c. alternative theories to the false consensus effect

   d. our tendency to believe that others think like us

2 What is the false consensus effect according to paragraph 1?

_____

3 What can be inferred from the experiment in paragraph 2?

   a. The researchers estimated how many subjects would carry a sandwich board.

   b. The subjects were given a reward if they agreed to carry the board.

   c. The rate of agreement was greater than that of disagreement among subjects.

   d. Those who refused the request assumed that other people would also refuse.

4 Which is NOT mentioned as a cause of the false consensus effect?

   a. We often assume how others think by considering the beliefs of people close to us.

   b. We have positive feelings about ourselves by believing others think like us.

   c. We do not change our beliefs easily once we have them.

   d. We pay more attention to the opinions that are similar to our own.

5 What is the best expression for blank (A)?

   a. you need evidence to persuade other people

   b. not everyone shares the same opinion

   c. your opinions are incorrect most of the time

   d. most people do not express their opinions openly

6 The sentence below is the first sentence of a short summary of the passage. Choose TWO additional sentences from below to complete the summary.

> The false consensus effect explains why we believe people have the same opinion as ours.

   a. The effect hasn't been proved by experiments yet.

   b. Our friends and family often think differently from us.

   c. We normally feel good when we believe others think like we do.

   d. We easily pay attention to different opinions from ours.

   e. The effect gets stronger when we have a firm belief.

WORD REVIEW TEST

[1~3] Choose the word that is closest in meaning to the underlined word.

1. Bacteria multiply quickly in moist environments.
    a. rest   b. move   c. reproduce   d. survive

2. The woman took her son to the doctor's office for a flu shot.
    a. drug   b. injection   c. symptom   d. prevention

3. The coach emphasized the importance of leadership.
    a. showed   b. mentioned   c. highlighted   d. ignored

[4~6] Connect the matching words in columns A and B.

A	B
4. treat •	• a. birth
5. give •	• b. a resistance
6. build up •	• c. infections

[7~10] Choose the best word to complete each sentence.

7. _____ diseases are ongoing, usually incurable illnesses.
    a. Chronic   b. Fake   c. Negative   d. Painful

8. The patient is being treated with _____ and closely monitored.
    a. pain   b. dizziness   c. antibiotics   d. infections

9. The quality of the dance performance was beyond my _____.
    a. solutions   b. choices   c. experiments   d. expectations

10. He taught us the _____ way to breathe when doing yoga.
    a. former   b. positive   c. proper   d. responsible

[11~14] Choose the correct word for each definition.

opposite   spread   expose   organism   specific   unpleasant

11. completely different:

12. a living thing, especially one that is very small:

13. particular; clearly identified:

14. causing bad feelings:

[1~3] Choose the word that is closest in meaning to the underlined word.

1. These days I have difficulty <u>recalling</u> a person's name.
   a. sharing   b. doubting   c. considering   d. remembering

2. The man has always <u>struggled</u> to escape poverty.
   a. tried   b. activated   c. predicted   d. supported

3. Feeding the animals in this zoo is <u>absolutely</u> not allowed.
   a. partially   b. nearly   c. completely   d. generally

[4~7] Connect the matching words in columns A and B.

A		B
4. pay •		• a. the campus
5. walk around •		• b. a memory
6. retrieve •		• c. a choice
7. make •		• d. attention

[8~10] Choose the best word to complete each sentence.

8. Arguments over the election _____ the people living in the town.
   a. divided   b. proved   c. reduced   d. discovered

9. I could _____ the change in her feelings by looking at her face.
   a. notice   b. refuse   c. suggest   d. agree

10. Climate change is a global _____ to be handled by international cooperation.
    a. assumption   b. theory   c. opinion   d. phenomenon

[11~12] Choose the correct definition of the underlined word in each sentence.

> **hold** *v.* **1.** to have something in hands or arms: *hold a bag* **2.** to have a meeting or event: *The festival will be held next month.* **3.** to be able to accommodate someone or something inside: *This room can hold 100 people.* **4.** to have an opinion about something: *hold religious beliefs*

11. Jamie will be <u>holding</u> his first photo exhibition. _____

12. A majority of people <u>hold</u> positive views on the movie. _____

WARM-UP QUESTION • Do you know which country ruled India as a colony?

Britain ruled India as a colony from the 18th century until the middle of the 20th century. As a British colony, the people of India suffered a lot. Indians had almost no power in their own country.

5　　One example of this unfair relationship was the cotton industry. Indians worked hard to grow and pick cotton. After it was picked, it was shipped to England, where it was spun into cloth by steam-powered machines. This cloth was then shipped back to India to be sold there. Cotton was cheap, but cloth was expensive.
10 Most Indians could not afford to buy the cloth made from their own cotton!

　　By the middle of the 20th century, most Indians wanted to be free from British control. At that time many independence groups were started. Some of these groups were against the use of violence in their struggle. The chosen symbol for their peaceful movement was the *charkha*—a cotton spinning wheel.

15　　As a means of protest against England, Gandhi, the leader of the nonviolent movement, made his clothes himself using a new kind of spinning wheel. This new machine was cheap enough for everyone to buy and small enough to carry from place to place. Gandhi taught Indians how to use it and encouraged its use. These machines became very popular, and Indians were able to spin cotton wherever they were. Often
20 Indians would use these machines in public places where the British could see them.

　　By spinning their own cloth, Indians showed that _____(A)_____. They did not need to depend on Britain. Nor did they need to depend on
25 weapons. Rather, they chose to gain their independence peacefully.

WORD FOCUS

◀ Collocations for

relationship

a **close** *relationship*
a **healthy** *relationship*
build a *relationship*
end a *relationship*

WORD CHECK

Choose the correct words for the blanks from the highlighted words in the passage.

1. _____ a country controlled by a more powerful country
2. _____ to be in control of a group of people or a country
3. _____ the act of trying to hurt or kill sb or damage sth
4. _____ the state of being politically free from control by another country
5. _____ to twist fibers into thread to make cloth

MAIN IDEA

1 **What is the best title for the passage?**

a. Another Lesson from History

b. Until the Day of Independence

c. What a Great Leader Left Behind

d. The Wheel of Peaceful Independence

DETAILS

2 **What happened to the cotton shipped to England according to paragraph 2?**

_____

3 **According to the passage, the new kind of spinning wheel was** _____.

a. often used in public places

b. difficult to carry

c. designed by the British

d. sold at a high price

4 **What is the best expression for blank (A)?**

a. they were skilled at making cloth

b. independence by peaceful means is the best way

c. they could invent a spinning wheel by themselves

d. they could take control of their own economy and future

5 **Which of the following is NOT true according to the passage?**

a. The relationship between Britain and India was unfair.

b. The cloth spun in England was too expensive for Indians to buy.

c. Every independence group used the *charkha* as their symbol.

d. The new, portable spinning wheel was very popular among Indians.

SUMMARY

6 **Use the words in the box to fill in the blanks.**

| rule   cloth   wheel   violent   cotton   weapon   peaceful |

India suffered a lot during its days under British _____ but managed to find a unique way to achieve independence. Indians picked _____, which was shipped to England and then resold to Indians as _____. Gandhi promoted his idea of _____ independence by encouraging people to use a new, cheap type of spinning _____. Indians used the machines to spin cotton anywhere. Rather than fight the British, they chose to become independent peacefully.

American Slavery

During the 1600s, many European settlers in North America made a living by growing tobacco, sugar, and cotton on plantations. These plantations were most common in the Southern states. For just 27 dollars, plantation owners there could buy an African slave. They made fortunes by keeping slaves and not paying them a penny for their labor.

5　　For over 200 years, thousands of slaves were shipped over from Africa and sold in slave markets every year. In 1807, the United States government passed the Act to Prohibit the Importation of Slaves in an effort to end the slave trade. Unfortunately, the law was not really kept, and slave traders continued to bring slaves to America. By 1860, there were about 4 million slaves in the Southern states.

10　　Life for slaves was very hard. ■ They did backbreaking work for long hours. ■ They were the property of their owners. ■ These children were slaves from the moment they were born till the day they died. ■ With such a system in place, it seemed that slavery would never end.

Despite the awful life of slaves, few tried to escape the plantations. Running away was 15 extremely dangerous, and very few succeeded. Slave owners would hunt them down using dogs. If the runaway was caught, he or she was badly beaten or even killed as an example to other slaves.

To be free, runaway slaves had to travel hundreds of miles to reach Canada, where slavery was illegal. They had to travel secretly, or they would be caught by the police and 20 sent back to the plantations. However, there was a small, secret organization called the Underground Railroad that helped the runaways by giving them food and a place to hide. It was a long and dangerous journey, but some slaves did make it to freedom.

1 According to paragraph 2, the Act to Prohibit the Importation of Slaves

(a) set a standard price for African slaves

(b) couldn't be established because of plantation owners

(c) encouraged slaves in the Southern states to escape

(d) wasn't powerful enough to put an end to the slave trade

2 Look at the four squares [■] that indicate where the following sentence could be added to the passage.

When they had children, they also belonged to the plantation owners.

Where would the sentence best fit?

3 In paragraph 3, the author suggests that slavery

ⓐ made slaves die young

ⓑ didn't allow slaves to keep property

ⓒ couldn't be escaped by the children of slaves

ⓓ encouraged slaves to have as many children as possible

4 The word illegal in the passage is closest in meaning to

ⓐ cruel   ⓑ proper   ⓒ official   ⓓ unlawful

5 According to paragraph 5, the Underground Railroad was

ⓐ a railway system used by slaves

ⓑ a police organization that looked for slaves

ⓒ a group of people who helped runaway slaves

ⓓ a hidden route connecting plantations to one another

6 Directions   Look at the sentence in bold. It is the first sentence of a short summary of the passage. Choose THREE answers to complete the summary. Wrong answer choices use minor ideas from the passage or use information that is not in the passage.

American plantation owners forced slaves to work for them between the 17th and 19th centuries.

ⓐ Slave traders made fortunes by bringing slaves to America.

ⓑ The US government's effort to stop the slave trade wasn't successful.

ⓒ The number of slaves escaping increased gradually.

ⓓ Slaves were not allowed to read or get an education.

ⓔ It was very difficult and dangerous for slaves to escape to freedom.

ⓕ A secret organization helped slaves who ran away from the plantations.

WORD REVIEW TEST

[1~3] Choose the word that is closest in meaning to the underlined word.

1.   Some adults continue to <u>depend on</u> their parents financially.
   a. belong to   b. believe in   c. deal with   d. rely on

2.   Smoking is <u>prohibited</u> inside the building.
   a. forbidden   b. left   c. hidden   d. encouraged

3.   I'm concerned that people doing <u>backbreaking</u> work are not paid enough.
   a. uninteresting   b. physical   c. stressful   d. exhausting

[4~6] Connect the matching words in columns A and B.

A	B
4. spin •	• a. control of
5. rule •	• b. cotton
6. take •	• c. a country

[7~10] Choose the best word to complete each sentence.

7.   Many studies show that _____ on TV leads to aggressive behavior.
   a. symbol   b. future   c. violence   d. trade

8.   Don't touch other people's _____ without permission.
   a. runaway   b. property   c. journey   d. freedom

9.   It is _____ to sell tobacco to someone under 20.
   a. illegal   b. expensive   c. enough   d. popular

10.   The celebrity is active in the _____ to protect animals.
   a. trader   b. example   c. movement   d. moment

[11~14] Choose the correct word for each definition.

public   fortune   slavery   importation   industry   plantation

11.   a large sum of money:

12.   the act of bringing something to a country from other countries:

13.   a large area of land where crops are grown:

14.   a field of business that provides a certain product or service:

UNIT 15

READING EXPERT

A 5-LEVEL READING COURSE for EFL Readers

2

NE _ Neungyule

Answers & Explanations

READING EXPERT

A 5-LEVEL READING COURSE for EFL Readers

2

Answers & Explanations

Reading 용어 및 지시문

I. 글의 구조와 관련된 용어

- **passage(지문):** 한 주제를 다룬 하나의 짧은 글을 말한다. 여러 개의 단락이 모여 한 지문을 구성한다.
- **paragraph(단락):** 글쓴이가 하나의 주제에 대하여 전개해 나가는 서로 연관된 여러 문장의 집합을 말한다. 흔히 들여쓰기로 단락과 단락 사이를 구분한다.
- **main idea(요지):** 글쓴이가 말하고자 하는 바, 즉 중심이 되는 견해로 보통 문장으로 표현된다.
- **topic sentence(주제문):** 글쓴이의 중심적 견해를 담고 있는 문장으로 각 단락에는 topic sentence가 있다.

II. 지시문

- **What is the best title for the passage?** (이 글에 가장 알맞은 제목은?)
- **What is the passage mainly about?** (이 글은 주로 무엇에 관한 내용인가?)
- **What is the main idea of the passage?** (이 글의 중심생각[요지]은 무엇인가?)
- **What is the best word [expression] for blank (A)?** (빈칸 (A)에 들어갈 말로 가장 알맞은 것은?)
- **What is the best pair for blanks (A) and (B)?** (빈칸 (A)와 (B)에 들어갈 말을 짝지은 것 중 가장 적절한 것은?)
- **Which is closest in meaning to <u>appreciated</u>?** (<u>appreciated</u>의 의미와 가장 가까운 것은?)
- **What does the underlined part mean?** (밑줄 친 부분이 의미하는 것은?)
- **What can be inferred from the underlined part?** (밑줄 친 부분에서 유추할 수 있는 것은?)
- **Which of the following is NOT mentioned in the passage?** (다음 중 이 글에서 언급되지 않은 것은?)
- **Which of the following is NOT true according to the passage?** (다음 중 본문의 내용과 일치하지 않는 것은?)
- **Write T if the statement is true or F if it's false.** (진술이 참이면 T, 거짓이면 F를 쓰시오.)
- **Where would the following sentence best fit?** (다음 문장이 들어갈 위치로 가장 알맞은 곳은?)
- **Use the words in the box to fill in the blanks.** (상자 안의 단어를 골라 빈칸을 채우시오.)
- **Match each topic to the correct paragraph in the passage.** (각 주제와 본문의 단락을 알맞게 연결하시오.)

UNIT 01.
Sports

WORD CHECK

1. disguise　2. disciplined　3. fierce　4. slavery
5. graceful

▶ fascinating: very interesting and attractive

정답

1. b　2. ⓒ　3. Because they (the government) feared that it could be used for violent crimes.　4. b　5. c
6. combination, developed, disguise, banned

해석

　　무술을 배울 계획이라면, 카포에이라는 어떨까? 카포에이라는 춤, 음악, 그리고 무술을 결합한 브라질의 한 예술 행위이다. 참가자들은 손뼉 치고, 노래하고, 악기를 연주하는 사람들이 이룬 원 안에서 공연한다. 그들은 서로를 때리지 않으면서 주먹을 날리고 발차기를 하며 매혹적인 춤을 만들어 낸다. 내가 처음 카포에이라를 배우기 시작했을 때 나는 그것의 힘 있는 동작과 우아한 움직임에 깊은 인상을 받았다. 그러나 나중에, 나는 그것이 다채롭고 흥미진진한 역사도 가지고 있다는 것을 이해하기 시작했다.

　　그것은 주로 16세기에, 아프리카에서 브라질로 끌려온 노예들에 의해 만들어졌다. 그들은 서로에게 싸우는 법을 가르치고 싶었지만 그들의 주인에게 이 행위를 숨겨야 했다. 그래서 그들은 그것을 춤의 한 형태로 위장했다. 오늘날 카포에이라 공연을 보면, 여러분은 아마 연주가들이 어떤 식으로 빠르기를 자주 바꾸는지 알아챌 것이다. 과거에, 이는 주인이 다가오고 있음을 알리고 카포에이라를 하는 사람들이 싸움 동작에서 춤 동작으로 바꾸도록 경고하기 위해 행해졌다.

　　1865년부터 1870년에 일어난 파라과이 전쟁 중에 많은 노예가 강제로 군대에 합류하게 되었다. 그들의 카포에이라 기술은 그들을 사나운 투사로 만들었고, 그 예술 행위는 많은 추종자를 얻게 되었다. 그러나 브라질에서 노예 제도가 종식된 직후인 1890년에, 정부는 카포에이라를 불법으로 규정했다. 그들은 그것이 폭력적인 범죄에 이용될까 봐 두려워했다. 카포에이라에 대한 금지는 1930년대에 철회되었고, 오늘날 그것은 브라질의 국기(國技) 중 하나이며, 그 어느 때보다 인기가 많다.

　　카포에이라는 보기에 아름다운 예술 행위이고, 참여하기에 재미있다. 게다가, 그것은 힘을 키우고, 유연성을 길러 주며, 여러분을 더 절제된 사람으로 만들어 준다. 나는 여러분 모두가 카포에이라를 한번 해 보길 적극 권장한다.

구문 해설

(4행) Participants perform inside a circle of people [who clap, sing, and play musical instruments].
▶ who는 people을 선행사로 하는 주격 관계대명사

(14행) In the past, this was done **to indicate** that ... and **to warn** the performers *to switch* ....

▶ to indicate, to warn은 목적을 나타내는 부사적 용법의 to부정사
▶ warn + 목적어 + to-v: ~이 …하도록 경고하다

(25행) I strongly **encourage** all of you **to** *give* capoeira *a try*.
▶ encourage + 목적어 + to-v: ~이 …하도록 권장하다
▶ give ~ a try: ~을 한번 해 보다

WORD FOCUS　chance

a fair chance 상당한 가능성 / little chance 희박한 가능성 / a fifty-fifty chance 반반의 확률 / ruin the chance(s) 가능성을 없애다[망치다]

WORD CHECK

1. equip　2. expedition　3. alternative
4. advantage　5. assistant

▶ trace: sth small that shows the existence or presence of sth else

정답

1. c　2. d　3. d　4. Because alpine-style climbers work quickly, leaving behind no trace of their amazing accomplishments.　5. assistants, equipment, carry, garbage

해석

　　세계에서 가장 높은 산을 오르는 것은 쉬운 일이 아니다. 하지만 그것을 '알파인 스타일'이라고 알려진 방식으로 하면 훨씬 더 어렵다. 이 일이 1975년에 라인홀트 메스너와 피터 하벨러가 하기로 결심했던 것이다.

　　알파인 스타일 등반은 아시아 히말라야산맥의 높은 산들을 오르는 전통적인 방법에 대한 대안으로 생겨났다. 전통적인 방식, 즉 포위 스타일에서는 등반가들이 수십 명의 보조를 고용해서 필요한 물품을 갖춘 일련의 캠프를 설치한다. 그리고 나서 그들은 한 캠프에서 다음 캠프로 올라가며, 마침내 산 정상에 도달하게 된다.

　　그러나 알파인 스타일은 필요한 모든 것을 등에 지고 한 번의 시도로 산을 오르는 것을 의미한다. 유럽의 알프스산맥에서 이름을 딴 것으로, 이 스타일에서는 등반가들이 산의 맨 밑에서 출발해야 한다. 그들은 고정된 로프를 사용하거나, 산소통을 가지고 가거나, 자신의 장비와 물품 운반을 도와줄 짐꾼을 고용할 수 없다.

　　메스너와 하벨러가 가셔브룸 1봉이라고 알려진 히말라야의 산을 이 방식으로 등반하려고 출발했을 때, 다른 등반가들은 그들이 미쳤다고 생각했다. 그들은 알파인 스타일은 더 조그만 산에 적합한 것이지, 히말라야산맥에는 맞지 않는다고 생각했다. 그러나 메스너와 하벨러는 모두가 틀렸다는 것을 증명했다. 그들이 가셔브룸 1봉 정상에 도달하는 데 단 3일이 걸렸고 그들은 알파인 스타일로 8,000미터 이상의 산을 오른 최초의 팀이 되었다.

위험성이 큰에도 불구하고, 알파인 스타일에는 몇 가지 장점이 있다. 시간이 덜 들기 때문에, 눈보라나 눈사태를 만날 확률이 더 낮다. 이 방식은 환경에도 더 좋다. 전통적인 스타일의 탐험에서는, 많은 캠프를 짓는 대규모의 등반 팀들이 찢어진 텐트나 빈 산소통 같은 쓰레기를 많이 남긴다. 그러나 알파인 스타일 등반가들은 신속히 작업하여 그들의 놀라운 성취의 흔적을 남기지 않는다.

구문 해설

3행 This is **what** Reinhold Messner and Peter Habeler decided to do in 1975.
▶ what은 선행사를 포함한 관계대명사

5행 The alpine style of climbing was developed as an alternative to the traditional way [the tall mountains of the Asian Himalayas were being climbed].
▶ the tall 이하는 the traditional way를 수식하는 관계부사절 (앞에 way가 쓰였으므로 관계부사 how는 생략됨)

13행 They cannot ┌ use fixed ropes,
├ bring along oxygen tanks,
├ or
└ hire porters **to help** carry ....
▶ to help는 porters를 수식하는 형용사적 용법의 to부정사

19행 **It took** them only three days **to reach** the top of Gasherbrum I ....
▶ It takes + A + 시간 + to-v: A가 ~하는 데 … 시간이 걸리다

UNIT 02.
Language

READING 1   p. 12~13

WORD FOCUS day

the following day 다음날 / the previous day 전날 / the very day 바로 그날 / the other day 일전에, 며칠 전에

WORD CHECK

1. transportation   2. watch over   3. stab   4. line
5. riddle
▶ multiple: being more than one

정답

1. c   2. d   3. b   4. (1) T (2) T (3) F   5. double, trains, sound, laugh, powerful

해석

해석

말장난은 소리나 형태가 비슷한 단어들을 사용함으로써 이중적인 의미를 만들어 낸다. 말장난은 하나 이상의 의미를 가진 단어들을 써서 만들어질 수도 있다. 말장난은 대개 사람들을 웃게 하려고 사용되지만, 사람들이 더 깊이 생각하도록 만들 수도 있다.

여러 가지 의미를 가진 단어들을 사용하는 말장난은 동형이의어 말장난이라고 알려져 있다. 한 가지 좋은 예를 다음 수수께끼에서 찾아볼 수 있다. 차장과 교사의 차이점은 무엇인가? 정답은 '차장은 기차(train)를 지키지만(mind), 교사는 정신(mind)을 교육한다(train).'이다. 이 경우에, 두 단어는 각기 두 개의 다른 의미를 지니고 있다. 동사로 'mind'는 '지키다'를 의미할 수 있다. 그러나 명사로 그것은 '정신'을 의미한다. 그리고 단어 'train'은 교통수단의 형태 또는 가르치는 행위를 가리킬 수 있다.

반면에, 동음이의어 말장난은 발음이 비슷하지만 다른 의미를 가진 두 단어를 사용한다. 예를 들어, 한 피자 가게의 간판에 'Seven days without pizza makes one weak. (피자가 없는 일주일은 사람을 약하게 만든다.)'라고 쓰여 있을지 모른다. 여기서, 'weak(약한)'이라는 단어는 'week(주)'라는 단어와 소리가 같아서 말장난이 만들어졌다. 7일은 실제로 정말 한 주를 구성하지만, 피자를 먹지 않는 것은 사람을 약하게 할 수 있다. 혹은 적어도 그것은 그 식당 주인이 당신들로 하여금 믿게 하고 싶은 말이다.

그러나 말장난은 가장 위대한 영문학 작품의 일부에도 사용되어 왔다. 예를 들어 〈로미오와 줄리엣〉에서 셰익스피어는 'Ask for me tomorrow, and you shall find me a grave man. (내일 나를 찾으면, 당신은 내가 진지한 사람/무덤에 있는 사람임을 알게 될 것이다.)'이라고 썼다. 이 대사는 막 칼에 찔린 후 머큐시오에 의해 읊어진다. 'grave'라는 단어가 '진지한'을 의미할 수 있지만, 여기에서 그것은 또한 곧 그가 죽을 것임을 암시한다. 이 예는 말장난이 흔히 그저 농담이지만, 글을 더 강렬하게 만드는 데에도 사용될 수 있음을 분명하게 보여 준다.

구문 해설

1행 Puns create a double meaning **by using** words [that *either* sound *or* look alike].
▶ by v-ing: ~함으로써
▶ either A or B: A나 B 둘 중 하나

4행 Puns are often used **to** *make* people *laugh*, but they can *make* people *think* more deeply as well.
▶ to make는 목적을 나타내는 부사적 용법의 to부정사
▶ make(사역동사) + 목적어 + 동사원형: ~을 …하게 만들다

16행 Seven days **do** indeed make one week, *while* not eating pizza can make a person weak.
　　　　　　　　　　　　　　S　　　　V　　O　　　OC
▶ 동사의 의미를 강조하기 위해 동사 make 앞에 조동사 do가 쓰임
▶ while은 '~이긴 하지만'이라는 의미로 쓰인 접속사

17행 Or at least that is **what** the restaurant owner wants you to believe.
▶ what은 '~하는 것'이라는 의미로 선행사를 포함한 관계대명사

4

READING 2 — p. 14~15

WORD FOCUS　guess

a lucky guess 운 좋게 맞힌 추측 / a wild guess 멋대로의 추측, 억측 / a rough guess 대강의 짐작 / make a guess 추측하다

WORD CHECK

1. variety　2. recognize　3. publish　4. distance
5. common

▶ accent: a unique way of pronouncing words

정답

1. a　2. They call it[a farm] a "station."　3. c　4. c
5. b　6. variety, native, confusing, recognize

해석

　　전 세계 인구 중 4억 명 이상이 영어 원어민이다. 이들 모두 영어를 쓰고는 있지만, 거리와 시간이 이 언어에 차이점들을 만들어냈다. 이 차이점들은 서로 다른 악센트에서부터 매우 다른 어휘까지 어떤 것이든 될 수 있다.

　　아침에 옷을 입는 미국 소년을 예로 들어 보자. 그는 underwear(속옷), pants(바지), sweater(스웨터)를 입고, socks(양말)와 running shoes(운동화)를 신는다. 이와 똑같은 옷을 입는 영국 소년은 underpants, trousers, jumper를 입고, socks와 trainers를 신는다. 미국 남학생은 high school(고등학교)에 가는데, 영국 남학생은 secondary school에 간다.

　　호주에서 사용되는 영어 또한 다르다. 호주인들은 다른 나라 영어 사용자들이 알아듣지 못할 수도 있는 어휘를 많이 쓴다. 그들은 캥거루를 'roo'라고 하고, 닭을 'chook'이라고 하며, 농장을 'station'이라고 한다. 미국인 또는 영국인 친구들은 만나면 "Hi!" 또는 "Hello!"라고 한다. 하지만 호주에서 흔한 인사말은 "G'day!"이다.

　　당연히 이런 차이점은 혼란을 일으킬 수 있는데, 특히 영어 사용 국가 간에 얼마나 많은 영화와 책, 텔레비전 프로그램이 공유되는지를 생각해 보면 말이다. 따라서, 영국 책이 미국에서 출판되기 전에 편집자들은 미국 독자들의 이해를 돕기 위해 많은 어휘와 철자를 바꾼다. 그러나 영화와 텔레비전 프로그램은 변경 없이 보여지기 때문에, 이따금 영어 원어민조차도 그것들을 이해하기 어려울 때가 있다.

　　그럼에도 불구하고 영국 영어, 미국 영어, 호주 영어 간의 여러 가지 차이점은 영어의 풍부함과 다양성을 보여 준다. 당신은 각 영어의 독특한 어휘를 배우는 일이 재미있다는 것을 알게 될 것이다. 조금만 연습하면 당신은 어떤 사람의 악센트와 어휘로부터 사람의 국적을 알아맞힐 수 있게 될 것이다. 하지만 조심해라! 만일 당신의 짐작이 틀리면 영국인을 'get angry(화나게)'하게, 미국인을 'get mad'하게, 호주인을 'go berko'하게 할 수도 있으니 말이다!

구문 해설

4행　Take the example of an American boy [**getting**
dressed in the morning].

9행　They **call** a kangaroo a "roo," a chicken a "chook,"
　　　V　　O₁　　OC₁　　O₂　　OC₂
and a farm a "station."
　　　O₃　　OC₃
▶ call A B: A를 B라고 부르다

19행　With a little practice, you will be able to guess a
　　　　(= If you practice a little)
speaker's country ....

21행　..., you could **make** a British person "**get** angry," an
　　　　　　　V　　O₁　　OC₁
American "**get** mad," or an Australian "**go** berko"!
　O₂　　OC₂　　　　O₃　　OC₃
▶ make(사역동사) + 목적어 + 동사원형: ~을 …하게 만들다

WORD REVIEW TEST

UNIT 01 — p. 16

1. b　2. c　3. a　4. d　5. b　6. a　7. d　8. c
9. crime　10. flexibility　11. alternative　12. equipped
13. illegal　14. attempt　15. participant　16. fixed

UNIT 02 — p. 17

1. d　2. b　3. a　4. c　5. a　6. b　7. b　8. a　9. d
10. d　11. verb　12. refer to　13. editor
14. conductor

UNIT 03.
Jobs

READING 1 — p. 18~19

WORD FOCUS　job

a temporary job 임시직 / get a job 직장[일]을 구하다 / lose a job 실직하다 / apply for a job 일자리에 지원하다

WORD CHECK

1. ensure　2. appear　3. sustainable
4. look through　5. skilled

▶ generation: a group of people in society who are born around the same time

정답

1. d 2. b 3. c 4. They are new technology and society's changing needs. 5. (1) collects (2) delivers (3) environment (4) behavior

해석

오늘날 당신이 친숙하게 여기는 직업의 다수가 최근까지는 사실 존재하지 않았다는 것을 알고 있었는가? 예를 들어, 업무가 스마트폰과 관련 있는 사람들을 생각해 보라. 스마트폰이 2000년대 중반에 인기를 끌 때까지, '앱 개발자' 또는 '앱 마케팅 담당자'는 없었다. 그러나 요즘, 수천 명의 사람이 이런 일들을 한다. 그러면 어떤 다른 종류의 직업들이 최근에 등장했을까?

가장 흔한 새로운 직업 중 하나는 '데이터 수집가'이다. 현대의 시장 조사는 고객 데이터에 크게 의존하기 때문에, 기업들은 그것을 모으고 분석하기 위해 전문가들을 고용하고 있다. 소비자 행동 동향을 파악하기 위해 많은 양의 고객 데이터를 검토하는 그 전문가들이 데이터 수집가이다. 그들의 도움으로 사업체들은 미래 동향을 예측하거나 맞춤형 광고를 제작할 수 있다.

최근에 생겨난 또 다른 직업은 '드론 조종사'이다. 드론은 오랫동안 존재해 왔지만, 그것들은 오직 군대나 취미로 그것들을 날리는 사람들에 의해 사용되었다. 그러나, 지금은 일부 대기업들이 드론을 그들의 사업의 일부로 만들고 있다. 예를 들면, 온라인 쇼핑 사이트들은 배송하는 데 그것들을 사용할 계획을 하고 있고, 영화 제작사들은 공중에서 장면들을 촬영하기 위해 이미 그것들을 사용하고 있다. 이 모든 기업들은 최첨단 드론을 조종하는 데 숙련된 사람들을 필요로 할 것이다.

물론, 새로운 기술이 직업 동향에 영향을 미치는 유일한 요인은 아니다. 사회의 변화하는 요구 역시 직업 시장을 형성하고 있다. 예를 들어, 이제 어떤 기업들은 그들의 사업 관행이 환경적인 면에서 지속 가능하도록 도와줄 '지속 가능성 전문가'를 고용하고 있다. 다른 기업들은 심지어 '젊은 세대 전문가'를 찾고 있다. 이들은 나이가 든 경영진에게 젊은 세대의 행동을 설명해 줄 수 있는 대개 젊은 사람들이다. 이와 같은 예들은 직업 동향이 빠르게 변화하고 있다는 것을 명확히 해 준다. 당신이 사회에 나갈 때쯤이면 어떤 종류의 직업들이 있을지 상상할 수 있겠는가?

구문 해설

1행 Did you know that many of the jobs [(**that**[**which**]) you *are familiar with* today] didn't actually exist until recently?

▶ you 앞에 목적격 관계대명사 that[which]이 생략됨

▶ be familiar with: ～에 익숙하다[익히 알다]

16행 Now, however, some big companies are **making** drones **part of their business**.

▶ make + 목적어 + 명사: ～을 …로 만들다

26행 Can you imagine {**what** kind of jobs will be available [*by the time* you go out into society]}?

▶ what 이하는 간접의문문으로 「의문사 + 주어 + 동사」의 어순

▶ by the time: ～할 때까지(는), ～할 때쯤이면

READING 2   p. 20~21

WORD CHECK

1. contain 2. brilliantly 3. display 4. creation
5. fragile

▶ multicolored: having many different colors

정답

1. b 2. Because he was amazed by (the skill of) glassblowing. 3. (1) ⓑ (2) ⓒ (3) ⓐ 4. a 5. b
6. (1) ⓒ (2) ⓑ (3) ⓔ (4) ⓐ (5) ⓓ

해석

데일 치훌리는 워싱턴 시애틀 출신의 유리 공예가이다. 대학에서 인테리어 디자인을 공부하던 어느 날, 치훌리는 glassblowing(유리세공)을 보게 되었다. 그는 이 기술에 놀라서 유리 공예가가 되기로 결심했다. 현재 그의 예술품은 전 세계 박물관과 공공건물에 전시되어 있고, 많은 나라 사람들이 그의 아름다운 유리 창작물을 매우 좋아한다. 나는 최근에 그의 작업실 근처에 있는 커피숍에서 그 예술가와 대화를 나누었다.

Q: 왜 유리를 가지고 예술 작품을 만들기로 결심하셨습니까?
Chihuly: 유리는 빛과 색을 아주 잘 보여 주기 때문에 매우 아름답습니다. 저는 그것을 여러 가지 다른 형태로 만들어 낼 수 있습니다. 또한, 유리는 매우 깨지기 쉽습니다. 아주 쉽게 깨질 수 있어서 매우 특별해 보입니다. 저는 화려하게 색을 입힌 유리로 여러 다른 모양과 크기의 작품을 만들어 냅니다.

Q: 유리 창작물에 대한 아이디어는 어디에서 얻으십니까?
Chihuly: 그것은 제 주변의 세상으로부터 나옵니다. 제 어머니의 아름다운 화원은 제게 영감을 줍니다. 또 저는 바다 근처에 사는데 바다가 제게 아이디어를 주기 때문에 해변을 따라 걷는 것도 아주 좋아합니다. 또한, 북미 원주민의 바구니나 담요 같은 다른 종류의 예술품에서 아이디어를 얻기도 합니다.

Q: 라스베이거스의 벨라지오 호텔에 만드신 유리 천장에 대해 말씀해 주시겠습니까?
Chihuly: 100명의 다른 분들의 도움으로 벨라지오 (호텔) 로비에 그 천장을 만들었습니다. 그것은 제가 지금까지 만든 것 중 제일 큰 작품이지요. 거기에는 다양한 색상을 지닌 천여 개의 유리 꽃이 금속 가지에 매달려 있습니다.

Q: 작품 작업을 보통 혼자 하십니까, 다른 사람들과 함께 하십니까?
Chihuly: 저는 영화감독 스타일로 일합니다. 제 작업실에서 유리 공예가 팀을 이끄는 것이지요. 각 공예가는 전문적으로 맡은 일이 있습니다. 우리는 제 디자인에 따라 작품을 만들기 위해 협업합니다. 그 일은 아주 멋진 과정이지요.

구문 해설

15행 I create pieces of many different shapes and sizes **out of** brilliantly colored glass.

▶ out of: (재료를 나타내어) ～으로

26행 Can you tell us about the glass ceiling [(that[which]) you created for the Bellagio Hotel ...]?

31행 It is **the largest** piece (that) I **have** ever **made**.
▶ 최상급 + (that) + 주어 + have (ever) p.p.: 이제까지 ~한 것 중에 가장 …한

32행 It contains about one thousand multicolored glass flowers [that hang from metal branches].

UNIT 04.
Society

READING 1
p. 22~23

WORD FOCUS weight

put on weight 체중이 늘다 / watch one's weight ~의 체중을 조절하다 / weight loss 체중 감량 / weight control 체중 조절

WORD CHECK

1. requirement   2. assistance   3. shelter   4. addict
5. branch
▶ financial: related to money

정답

1. c   2. The benefits include financial aid, housing assistance, and access to employment opportunities.
3. b   4. d   5. c   6. homeless, employment, branches, enrolling

해석

새벽 5시 30분, 텅 빈 주차장에 한 무리의 사람들이 아침 조깅을 위해 모인다. 그러나 그들은 체중을 줄이거나 마라톤 연습을 위해 조깅을 하는 것이 아니다. 그들은 노숙자들이며, 그들 중 많은 이가 자신들의 삶을 개선하기 위해 노력하는 이전의 마약, 알코올 중독자들이다.

그들은 Back on My Feet이라는 단체의 회원이다. 회원들은 일주일에 세 번 단체 달리기를 한다. 유일한 요건은 그들이 그 단체에 합류하기 전에 적어도 한 달간, 마약을 하거나 술을 마시지 않아야 한다는 것이다. 즐기며 운동을 할 뿐만 아니라, 회원들은 30일 후에 유용한 혜택도 얻는다. 이것들에는 재정적인 도움, 주거지 지원, 고용 기회가 포함된다.

Back on My Feet은 2007년에 시작되었는데, 그 당시 앤 말콤은 필라델피아의 노숙자 쉼터에 달리기 클럽을 조직하기로 했다. 많은 사람이 그녀의 생각은 절대로 성공하지 못할 거라고 그녀에게 말했다. "사람들이 '이들은 뛰길 원하지 않을 겁니다. 그들은 다른 걱정거리들이 있어요.'라 말했

죠."라고 그녀는 설명한다. 그러나 그들은 분명히 틀렸다. 단 6년 만에, 그 클럽은 10개 도시에 회원이 거의 4백 명에 달하는 클럽으로 확대되었고, 2019년까지 미국 전역에 총 13개 도시로 퍼져나갔다.

Back on My Feet의 뉴욕 지부에는 현재 달리기 클럽에 약 60명의 회원이 있다. 그 지부는 첫해에 41명의 사람이 일자리를 찾는 것을 도왔고, 34명의 사람들이 거주지를 찾는 것을 도왔으며, 50명의 사람들을 직업 훈련 과정에 등록시켰다. 아침 조깅이 Back on My Feet 회원들의 주요 활동이겠지만, 그것은 바로 그들의 삶을 다시 정상 궤도로 돌려놓는 첫걸음이다.

구문 해설

3행 But they are not jogging **to lose** weight or **to train** for a marathon.
▶ to lose와 to train은 목적을 나타내는 부사적 용법의 to부정사

4행 ..., and many of them are former drug and alcohol addicts [**trying to improve** their lives].
▶ try to-v: ~하기 위해 노력하다

8행 The only requirement is [**that** they must be clean and sober ...].
▶ that이 이끄는 명사절이 주격보어 역할을 함

19행 ..., it **helped** 41 people **find** jobs, *assisted* 34 people *in finding* places to live, ...
▶ help + 목적어 + (to)-v: ~이 …하도록 돕다
▶ assist + 목적어 + in v-ing: ~이 …하는 것을 돕다

READING 2
p. 24~25

WORD FOCUS inspire

motivate 동기를 부여하다 / encourage 격려하다, 용기를 북돋우다 / influence 영향을 끼치다, 감화를 주다

WORD CHECK

1. instrument   2. immediately   3. landfill
4. recyclable   5. poverty
▶ material: a type of matter such as plastic or metal that is used for making things

정답

1. a   2. c   3. b   4. It is teaching them how to play music and how to build recycled instruments of their own.   5. (1) T (2) T (3) F   6. education, landfill, build, change

"세상은 우리에게 쓰레기를 보내죠. 우리는 음악을 돌려보냅니다."
– 파비오 차베스

　파라과이의 카테우라라는 마을은 쓰레기 매립지에 지어졌다. 인구의 대부분은 마을로 매일 가져다지는 쓰레기에서 재활용이 가능한 물품들을 수거하여 생계를 꾸려 간다. 가난 외에도, 카테우라의 사람들이 직면하고 있는 또 다른 난관은 교육의 부족이다. 그곳의 아이들 중 40%는 학교를 졸업하지 못한다. 이 아이들은 보통 일하기 위해 쓰레기 매립지로 보내진다.

　카테우라의 아이들에게 더 나은 미래를 주기 위해서, 파비오 차베스와 니콜라스 고메스라는 두 남자는 어린이 오케스트라를 만들기를 원했다. 그러나, 악기들이 너무 비쌌다. 어느 날, 파비오와 니콜라스에게 방안이 떠올랐다. 그 방안은 판금 조각들, 기름통, 밧줄, 그리고 빗자루들과 같은 쓰레기 매립지에서 발견된 재료들로 그들의 악기를 만드는 것이었다. 그렇게 '카테우라 재활용 오케스트라'가 탄생하게 되었다.

　그 오케스트라는 오직 몇 명의 연주자들로 시작했다. 그러나 그것은 35명 이상의 단원으로 확장되었다. 그것은 현재 200명 이상의 아이들에게 음악을 연주하는 방법과 심지어 그들 자신의 재활용 악기를 만드는 방법을 가르치고 있다. 이 오케스트라가 배고픔과 빈곤과 같은 문제들을 즉시 해결할 수는 없지만, 그것이 제공하는 교육은 미래에는 이러한 문제들을 직면하는 아이들의 수를 더 줄일 것이다.

　재활용 오케스트라에 의해 영감을 받아서, 스페인, 브라질, 그리고 멕시코와 같은 다른 나라의 사람들도 그들만의 재활용 오케스트라를 시작했다. 재활용 오케스트라는 카테우라의 거주민들에게 희망과 자부심을 가져다주었을 뿐만 아니라, 음악이 진실로 사회를 변화시킬 수 있는 힘을 가진다는 것을 보여 주었다.

구문 해설

13행 　It is now **teaching** more than 200 children *how*
　　 S　　　　V　　　　　　　　　IO
　to play music and even *how to build* recycled
　　　　　　　　　　　　　　　　DO
　instruments of their own.
　▶ teach + 간접목적어 + 직접목적어: ~에게 …을 가르치다
　▶ how to-v: ~하는 방법

15행 　..., the education [**that** it provides] will lead to fewer
　children [*facing* these problems in the future].
　▶ that은 the education을 선행사로 하는 목적격 관계대명사
　▶ facing 이하는 fewer children을 수식하는 현재분사구

17행 　**(Being) Inspired** by the Recycled Orchestra, people
　in other countries, ..., started their own recycled
　orchestras.
　▶ Inspired by the Recycled Orchestra는 원인을 나타내는 분사구문으로 앞에 Being이 생략됨

20행 　***Not only*** has the Recycled Orchestra brought hope
　and a sense of pride to the residents of Cateura, *but*
　it has *also* shown [**that** music truly has the power to
　change society].

　▶ 부정어 Not only가 문장 맨 앞으로 나오면서 주어와 조동사 (has)가 도치됨
　▶ not only A but also B: A뿐만 아니라 B도
　▶ 접속사 that 이하는 동사 has shown의 목적어 역할

WORD REVIEW TEST

1. d　2. a　3. c　4. d　5. b　6. d　7. a　8. c
9. advertising　10. executive　11. fragile
12. amazed　13. ceiling　14. analyze　15. director
16. film

1. b　2. b　3. d　4. c　5. b　6. a　7. enroll
8. inspire　9. provide　10. expanded　11. 3　12. 1

UNIT 05.
Animals

WORD FOCUS　mild

gentle 온화한 / temperate 온난한, 온대성의 / warm 따뜻한 / moderate 온화한

WORD CHECK

1. breed　2. ecosystem　3. fertile　4. erode
5. vegetation
▶ construction: the process of building or repairing sth such as a road or building

정답

1. d　2. (1) F (2) T (3) F　3. Because they had to compete with the rabbits for food and habitat.　4. c
5. c　6. bred, decreased, control, fences

해석

　토끼들은 위험할까? 대부분의 장소에서, 대답은 아니요이다. 그것들은 보통 귀엽고 사랑스럽다고 여겨지고, 많은 사람들은 그것들을 집에서 애완동물로 기른다. 그러나 호주에서, 토끼들은 그 나라의 민감한 생태계에 위협이 된다는 사실 때문에 큰 문제이다.

토끼들은 호주의 토착 동물이 아니었다. 그러나, 1859년에 한 남자가 24마리의 야생 토끼를 영국으로부터 호주의 빅토리아로 들여와서 그것들이 사냥될 수 있도록 숲에 풀어놨다. 불행하게도, 호주는 풍부한 공터와 먹을 수 있는 많은 식물이 있고, 사람들은 거의 없기 때문에 토끼들에게 완벽한 서식지이다. 또한, 호주의 겨울은 온화해서, 토끼들은 일 년 내내 번식할 수 있다. 가장 중요한 것은, 호주에는 토끼들의 자연적 포식자가 적다는 것이다.

곧 빅토리아에는 수백만 마리의 토끼들이 있게 되었다. 호주 땅의 대부분은 식량을 재배하는 데 알맞지 않고, 토끼들은 이 상황을 더욱더 나쁘게 만들었다. 그것들은 너무나 많은 식물들을 먹어 버려서 그 밑의 흙이 바람에 침식되었고 땅은 더욱 황폐해졌다. 게다가, 먹이와 서식지를 놓고 그 토끼들과 경쟁해야 했던 일부 토종 동물들은 그 개체 수가 크게 줄었다. 곧, 토끼들은 전국으로 퍼지기 시작했다. 1920년대 경에는, 호주 토끼의 개체 수가 대략 100억 마리로 추정되었다.

호주 정부는 토끼 개체 수를 통제하기 위해서 많은 것을 시도해 왔다. 20세기 초에는, 토끼들이 농지에 가지 못하게 막기 위해서 긴 울타리를 세웠다. 정부의 예상과는 달리, 많은 토끼들이 울타리 공사 중에 반대편으로 건너갔고, 다른 토끼들은 울타리 밑에 구멍을 팠다. 정부는 또한 토끼를 죽이는 질병들도 들여왔다. 이것은 토끼 개체 수를 크게 감소시켰지만, 오직 특정 지역에만 해당되었다.

오늘날, 호주의 토끼 개체 수는 약 2억 마리로 추정된다. 상황이 나아지기는 했지만, 그것은 여전히 호주가 필사적으로 해결하고자 하는 심각한 문제이다.

구문 해설

4행 But in Australia, rabbits are a big problem, **due to the fact** *that* they are a danger to the country's
delicate ecosystem.
  ▶ due to + 명사 : ~ 때문에
  ▶ that이 이끄는 절은 the fact와 동격 관계

14행 They ate **so** many plants **that** the soil underneath was eroded by the wind, *leaving* the land **even** less fertile.
  ▶ so ~ that ...: 너무 ~해서 …하다
  ▶ leaving 이하는 연속상황을 나타내는 분사구문
  ▶ even: 훨씬 (비교급 강조)

20행 ..., they built long fences **to** *keep* the rabbits *away from* farmland.
  ▶ to keep은 목적을 나타내는 부사적 용법의 to부정사
  ▶ keep + 목적어 + away from: ~이 …에 가까이 가지 못하게 하다

25행 Although the situation has improved, it is still a serious problem [**that** the country is desperately trying to solve].
  ▶ that은 a serious problem을 선행사로 하는 목적격 관계대명사

READING 2　TOEFL　　　　　　p. 30~31

정답

1. c　2. the fourth square　3. d　4. c　5. a
6. c, d, f

해석

아메리카들소

아메리카들소는 북미에서 가장 큰 육지 동물이다. 수컷은 무게가 2,000파운드까지 나가고 키가 1.8미터나 된다. 아메리카들소는 커다란 머리, 등에 난 혹, 길고 헝클어진 흑갈색 털을 가지고 있다. 아메리카들소는 먹을 풀을 찾아 무리 지어 함께 다닌다.

한때 거대한 (규모의) 아메리카들소 떼가 북미의 초원 지대를 누볐다. 그것들은 초원 지대에 사는 북미 원주민들에게 중요한 자원이었다. 그들은 아메리카들소를 사냥하여 이 동물의 거의 모든 부분을 이용했다. 고기는 먹고 뼈로는 연장과 무기를 만들었다. 담요, 옷, 텐트 모두가 아메리카들소의 가죽으로 만들어졌다. 아메리카들소는 또한 북미 원주민의 영적인 믿음에도 중요한 것이었다. 아메리카들소의 새끼는 4월에 태어나는데, 북미 원주민들은 친절한 정령이 그들이 생존할 수 있도록 도우려고 매년 봄에 그들에게 아메리카들소를 보내 주는 것이라고 믿었다.

이 모든 것은 1800년대에 유럽인들의 등장으로 변했다. 북미 원주민들은 자원이 필요할 때만 아메리카들소를 사냥했다. 반면에 유럽인들은 재미 삼아 그것들을 엄청나게 많이 죽였다. 그들은 하루 만에 누가 가장 많은 동물을 죽일 수 있는지 알아보기 위해 경쟁했다. 이것이 환경에 미친 영향은 엄청났다. 콜럼버스가 미국에 도착했을 때는 약 6,000만 마리의 아메리카들소가 있었다. 1890년경에는 1,000마리도 안 되는 숫자가 생존해 있었다.

아메리카들소는 아메리카들소 협회에 의해 멸종 위기를 모면했는데, 그 협회는 1905년에 생겨났다. 많은 수가 보호 지역에서 사육되었고 그 후 국립 공원에 풀어졌다. 오늘날에는 약 50만 마리가 있다. 아메리카들소는 여전히 보호되어야 할 필요는 있지만 더 이상 멸종 위기에 처해 있지 않다.

아메리카들소가 더 이상 북미 초원 지대에서 자유롭게 살 수는 없지만, 그것은 여전히 미국 서부 개척 시대의 상징이다. 해마다 국립 공원을 찾는 수천 명의 방문객들은 아메리카들소 떼를 보며 과거를 상상해 볼 수 있다.

구문 해설

3행 Bison travel together in herds **looking for** grass *to eat*.
  ▶ looking for 이하는 동시동작을 나타내는 분사구문
  ▶ to eat은 grass를 수식하는 형용사적 용법의 to부정사

8행 ..., and the native Americans believed [**that** a kind spirit sent them bison each spring *to help* them survive].
  S　　V　　S'
  V'　IO　DO
  ▶ that이 이끄는 명사절이 believed의 목적어로 쓰임
  ▶ to help는 목적을 나타내는 부사적 용법의 to부정사
  ▶ help + 목적어 + (to)-v: ~이 …하도록 돕다

9

They competed **to see** [*who* could kill the most animals in one day].

▶ to see는 목적을 나타내는 부사적 용법의 to부정사

▶ who 이하는 간접의문문으로 「의문사 + 주어 + 동사」의 어순임 (여기서는 who가 의문사이자 주어)

19행 Even though the bison can **no longer** live freely ....

▶ no longer: 더 이상 ~이 아닌

UNIT 06.
Literature

READING 1
p. 32~33

WORD FOCUS mystery

remain a mystery 수수께끼로 남아 있다 / be a mystery to sb ~에게 미스터리이다[의문으로 남다] / a complete mystery 완전한 수수께끼 / an unsolved mystery 풀리지 않은 미스터리

WORD CHECK

1. storyline   2. villain   3. witness   4. companion
5. faithful

▶ observant: able to notice many things

정답

1. b   2. a   3. Because the storyline is usually focused on discovering who the villain actually is.   4. c
5. amateur, solve, errors, identified

해석

대부분의 추리 소설과 이야기들은 동일한 기본 줄거리를 공유한다. 단서를 찾고, 증인을 심문하고, 범인의 정체를 알아냄으로써 풀려야 하는 미스터리가 있다는 것이다. 또한, 추리 소설에는 반복적으로 나타나는 많은 전형적인 등장인물 유형이 있다.

이런 이야기들의 영웅들은 거의 항상 일종의 탐정이다. 탐정은 전문가나 비전문가일 수 있지만, 그 사람은 매우 현명하고, 관찰력이 있으며, 논리적이어야 한다. 탐정은 이러한 자질들을 이야기를 읽고 있는 사람과 함께 범죄를 해결하는 데 사용한다.

이 탐정들에게는 종종 그들을 돕는 충실한 조수가 있다. 이런 등장인물은 셜록 홈스의 믿음직한 친구의 이름을 따서 종종 '왓슨'이라 불린다. 그 사람은 보통 탐정만큼 현명하거나 논리적이지 않으며 종종 어리석은 실수를 저지른다. 그러나 왓슨 캐릭터는 여전히 탐정이 범죄를 해결하는 것을 어떻게든 돕는다.

마지막으로, 모든 잘 짜인 추리 소설에는 악당이 있어야 한다. 줄거리는 보통 이 사람이 실제로 누구인지를 밝히는 데 초점이 맞추어져 있다. 이런 이유로, 대부분의 경우에 악당의 실체는 소설의 마지막에 가서야 밝혀진다. 왓슨 캐릭터와 달리, 악당은 대개 탐정만큼이나 똑똑하다. 그러나 그 사람은 항상 한 가지 중대한 실수를 저지르고 결국 체포된다.

다음에 추리 소설을 읽을 때, 이 등장인물들이 어떻게 묘사되었는지 생각해 보아라. 그러나 미스터리를 풀어보는 것도 잊지 마라! 그것이 추리 소설을 읽는 데 있어 가장 재미있는 부분이니까!

구문 해설

1행 There is a mystery [that must be solved by
  — uncovering clues,
  — questioning witnesses,
  — and
  — discovering the identity of the criminal].

7행 The detective uses these qualities **to solve** the crime along with the person [who is reading the story].

▶ to solve는 목적을 나타내는 부사적 용법의 to부정사

9행 This character **is** sometimes **referred to as** a "Watson," after ....

▶ refer to A as B: A를 B라고 부르다 (수동태: A be referred to as B)

10행 He or she is generally **not as** wise and logical **as** the detective ....

▶ not as + 형용사/부사의 원급 + as: ~만큼 …하지 않은[않게]

13행 The storyline is usually focused on discovering [**who** this person actually is].

▶ who 이하는 간접의문문으로 「의문사 + 주어 + 동사」의 어순

READING 2
p. 34~35

WORD FOCUS lifelong

temporary 일시적인, 임시의 / transitory 일시적인, 잠깐의 / momentary 순간적인, 찰나의

WORD CHECK

1. overlook   2. recommend   3. stimulate
4. recognize   5. contribution

▶ literature: writing such as novels, poetry, plays, etc. which people consider important

정답

1. b   2. (1) T (2) F   3. They need the ability to see the world from a child's point of view and to stimulate children's imaginations.   4. c   5. c   6. (1) attention (2) recognizes (3) illustrator (4) lifelong (5) nationalities

해석

아이들은 재미있고 흥미로운 이야기들을 즐기고, 독서는 그들의 뇌가 발달하는 것을 돕는다. 하지만 독자들은 어떻게 최고의 아동 도서들을 찾을 수 있을까? 한 가지 방법은 주요 상들의 수상 작품들을 찾아보는 것이다. 아동 문학에 대한 많은 상들이 있다. 그러나, 가장 큰 두 개의 상은 뉴베리상과 한스 크리스티안 안데르센상이다.

뉴베리상은 1922년부터 매년 수여되어왔다. 그것은 책 판매상이자 편집자인 프레더릭 G. 멜처에 의해 시작되었다. 그 당시에는, 아동 문학이 흔히 간과되었다. 멜처는 그의 상이 아동 도서에 대한 대중적인 관심을 불러일으키고 사서들이 아이들에게 좋은 책들을 추천하는 것을 더 쉽게 만들어 주기를 희망했다. 그는 '아동 문학의 아버지'로 여겨지는 18세기의 영국 출판업자 존 뉴베리의 이름을 따서 그 상의 이름을 지었다. 수상작에는 로이스 라우리의 〈기억 전달자〉와 린다 수 박의 〈사금파리 한 조각〉이 있다.

한스 크리스티안 안데르센상은 아동 문학에 대한 유명한 작가의 기여를 기리기 위해서 1956년에 시작되었다. 그것은 2년마다 아동 도서 분야에서 한 명의 작가와 한 명의 삽화가에게 수여된다. 작품의 질과 더불어, 그 상의 심사 위원들은 각 후보자의 아이의 관점에서 세상을 보는 능력과 아이들의 상상력을 자극하는 능력을 고려한다. 몇몇 잘 알려진 과거 수상자들에는 유명한 〈무민〉 책의 작가인 토베 얀손과 〈마녀 배달부 키키〉의 작가인 카도노 에이코가 있다.

이 두 상 모두 매우 존경받지만, 그들 사이에는 몇 가지 큰 차이점들이 있다. 뉴베리상은 그해 최고의 아동 도서를 인정한다. 반면에, 안데르센상은 한 권의 책에만 근거하지 않는다. 그것은 상을 받는 사람들의 일생 동안의 업적을 기린다. 또한, 안데르센상은 모든 국적의 작가와 삽화가들을 고려하는 반면, 뉴베리상은 오직 미국의 시민이나 거주자들에게만 주어진다.

구문 해설

[3행] One way is **to look up** the winners of major awards.
▶ to look up은 be동사(is)의 보어로 쓰인 명사적 용법의 to부정사로 '~하는 것'으로 해석

[10행] Melcher hoped his award would **bring** public attention **to** children's books and make *it* easier **for librarians** *to recommend* good books to kids.
▶ bring A to B: B에게 A를 가져다주다
▶ it은 가목적어, to recommend 이하가 진목적어이며, for librarians는 to부정사의 의미상의 주어

[11행] He **named** the award **after** John Newbery, an 18th-century English publisher [*considered* the "father of children's literature]."
▶ name A after B: B의 이름을 따서 A의 이름을 짓다
▶ considered 이하는 an 18th-century English publisher를 수식하는 과거분사구

[17행] ..., the award's judges consider the ability of ...
to see the world from a child's point of view
and
to stimulate children's imaginations.

▶ to see와 to stimulate는 the ability를 수식하는 형용사적 용법의 to부정사

WORD REVIEW TEST

UNIT 05   p. 36

1. b   2. b   3. b   4. a   5. b   6. d   7. a   8. c
9. estimated   10. saved   11. released   12. eroded
13. hump   14. delicate   15. weapon   16. resource

UNIT 06   p. 37

1. a   2. a   3. c   4. b   5. c   6. a   7. b   8. d
9. a   10. d   11. identity   12. capture   13. standard
14. judge

UNIT 07.
Environment

READING 1   p. 38~39

WORD FOCUS   feature

trait 특성 / quality 특질, 특성 / characteristic 특징

WORD CHECK

1. primary   2. adjust   3. solar   4. fertilizer
5. standard
▶ steady: continuing or without stopping

정답

1. a   2. c   3. ⓒ   4. Blinds on the outside of the windows automatically adjust depending on the angle of the sun.   5. b   6. stairs, adjusting, insulation, rainwater, fertilizer

해석

오늘날, 점점 더 많은 건축가들이 효율성과 지속 가능성을 염두에 두고 건물을 설계함에 따라, 건축이 '친환경적'이 되고 있다. 한 가지 훌륭한 예는 미국 워싱턴주의 시애틀에 있는 6층짜리 사무실 건물인 불릿 센터이다. 이 인상적인 건물은 그것이 사용하는 것보다 더 많은 에너지를 생산하고, 지속 가능한 건축의 새로운 기준이다.

불릿 센터는 2013년 4월 22일, 지구의 날에 문을 열었다. 그것의 주된 목적은 지속 가능성을 추구하는 사무실 건물들에 좋은 본보기가 되는 것

이다. 그 건물은 많은 친환경적인 특징들을 가지고 있다. 예를 들어, 자전거를 위한 차고는 있지만 자동차를 위한 차고는 없다. 또한, 지붕의 태양광 전지판은 그 건물의 모든 에너지를 공급한다. 또 다른 예로, 엘리베이터가 보이지 않는 곳에 위치해 있고 계단은 도시의 아름다운 경관을 제공하는데, 이것은 사람들이 계단을 이용하도록 장려한다.

여름철에는, 창문 밖의 블라인드가 건물 내부의 온도를 관리하기 위해 태양의 각도에 따라서 자동으로 조정된다. 추운 겨울날에는 특별한 열 펌프 시스템이 땅 깊은 곳으로부터 열을 흡수한다. 그런 다음 그 시스템이 이 열을 건물 안으로 전달하고 그와 동시에 삼중창이 환상적인 단열 기능을 제공한다.

불릿 센터의 지붕에는 빗물을 모으는 구멍들이 있다. 이 물은 지하의 탱크에 저장되고 건물 전체에서 사용된다. 비록 이 건물은 하루에 단지 약 500갤런의 물을 사용하지만, 그 탱크는 56,000갤런까지 저장할 수 있다! 마지막으로, 불릿 센터는 사람의 배설물을 비료로 바꾸는 특별한 화장실 시스템을 가지고 있다.

이러한 놀라운 특징들 덕분에, 불릿 센터는 앞으로 250년 동안 자체적으로 물과 전기의 지속적인 공급을 확보할 것이고 공과금 고지서를 피할 것이다! 그 건물의 건축가들은 그 건물이 다른 사람들로 하여금 친환경적 건축을 받아들이고 지속 가능성을 위한 실질적인 행동을 취하도록 고무하기를 희망한다.

구문 해설

6행
Its primary purpose is **to be** a good model for office buildings [*pursuing* sustainability].
- to be는 be동사(is)의 보어로 쓰인 명사적 용법의 to부정사
- pursuing 이하는 office buildings를 수식하는 현재분사구

9행
For another thing, the elevator is located **out of sight** and the stairway offers beautiful views of the city, *which* encourages people to take the stairs.
- out of sight: 보이지 않는 곳에, 먼 곳에
- which는 앞 절 전체를 선행사로 하는 계속적 용법의 관계대명사

11행
In summertime, blinds on the outside of the windows automatically adjust **depending on** the angle of the sun *to manage* the temperature inside the building.
- depending on: ~에 따라서
- to manage는 목적을 나타내는 부사적 용법의 to부정사

24행
The building's creators hope [**that** it will *inspire* others ┌ *to embrace* green architecture / and / └ (*to*) *take* practical action for sustainability].
- that이 이끄는 절은 동사 hope의 목적어 역할
- inspire + 목적어 + to-v: ~을 고무하여 …하게 하다

WORD FOCUS　ignore

overlook 간과하다, 못 본 체하다 / neglect 방치하다, 도외시하다 / disregard 무시하다

WORD CHECK

1. hive　2. dramatically　3. electromagnetic
4. extinct　5. pollinate

▶ depend on: to need sb or sth, especially to survive or be successful in specific circumstances

정답

1. b　2. b　3. d　4. We wouldn't be able to grow enough food to feed ourselves.　5. decreasing, potential, confuse, Toxic, pollinate

해석

기자: 안녕하십니까, 커클랜드 박사님. 최근 세계의 벌꿀 개체 수가 급격히 감소하고 있습니다. 이상하게도, 아무도 이유를 확실히 모릅니다. 이 상황을 설명해 주시겠습니까?

커클랜드 박사: 그러죠. 1970년대 이후로 북아메리카의 야생 꿀벌 수가 급속도로 감소해 오고 있습니다. 하지만 현재 우리는 양봉가들이 기르는 꿀벌 숫자에서도 비슷한 감소 추세를 목격하고 있습니다.

기자: 그렇군요. 가능한 원인으로 무엇이 있습니까?

커클랜드 박사: 가장 가능성 있는 원인은 기후 변화입니다. 꿀벌은 꽃에 의존해 사는데, 많은 식물들의 성장 시기가 기후에 따라 함께 변화하고 있습니다. 과학자들은 이것이 꿀벌에 어떤 식으로 영향을 미치는지를 알아내기 위해 노력하고 있습니다. 또한 우리의 휴대 전화기가 문제라고 생각하는 일부 연구자들도 있습니다. 이러한 전화기는 전자파를 사용하는데, 이것이 꿀벌을 교란시키고 있을 수 있습니다. 꿀벌들은 자신의 벌집으로 돌아가는 길을 찾지 못할 경우, 대부분 죽을 가능성이 높습니다. 그리고 마지막으로, 몇몇 과학자들은 식물에 뿌려지는 일부 살충제 안에 있는 유독한 화학 물질이 꿀벌을 죽게 한다고 믿습니다.

기자: 흥미롭군요. 그런데 사람들이 왜 신경을 써야 할까요? 꿀벌이 없으면, 꿀을 구하지 못하겠지요. 하지만 분명 걱정해야 할 더 큰 문제가 있을 텐데요.

커클랜드 박사: 꿀벌은 단순히 꿀 그 이상을 책임지고 있습니다. 실제로, 일부 전문가들은 만약 벌이 멸종된다면, 인간도 그렇게 될 것으로 생각합니다. 이는 벌들이 콩이나 사과, 브로콜리를 비롯한 거의 백여 가지의 다양한 작물을 수분시키기 때문입니다. 우리 식단의 3분의 1이 곤충이 수분하는 식물에서 비롯된다고 추정됩니다. 꿀벌이 없다면 우리가 먹을 만큼의 충분한 식량을 재배하지 못할 수도 있습니다.

기자: 알겠습니다. 분명 이것은 간과해서는 안 될 문제이군요. 정말 감사합니다, 커클랜드 박사님.

4행 **Ever since** the 1970s, *the number of* wild honeybees in North America **has been dropping** rapidly.

▶ ever since: ~이후로 줄곧

▶ the number of + 복수명사: ~의 수 (*cf.* a number of: 많은 ~)

▶ have been v-ing: 현재완료 진행형 (과거부터 현재까지 계속되고 있는 일을 나타냄)

9행 Scientists are trying to find out [**what** kind of effect this is having on honeybees].

▶ what 이하는 find out의 목적어 역할을 하는 간접의문문

12행 If they can't **find** their **way back to** their hive, they'll most likely die.

▶ find one's way back to: ~으로 돌아가는 길을 찾다

15행 **Without** honeybees, we'd **have** no honey.

▶ 「without + 명사, 주어 + would[could] + 동사원형」은 '~이 없다면 …할 텐데'라는 의미의 가정법 과거

18행 ... **if** bees **were to** go extinct, *so would* humans.

V S

▶ 가정법 과거 문장에서 if절에 were to를 사용하여 미래에 실현 가능성이 희박한 일을 나타낼 수 있음

▶ '~도 그렇다'라는 의미로 so가 강조되어 절의 맨 앞으로 나오면서 주어와 동사가 도치됨

UNIT 08.
Culture

READING 1   p. 42~43

WORD CHECK

1. weapon   2. consumer   3. variety   4. trade
5. practice

▶ infuser: a device that allows the flavor of tea to go into water

정답

1. b   2. b   3. It started as a result of trade with China.
4. a   5. a   6. (1) ⓐ (2) ⓐ (3) ⓑ

해석

　많은 영국인에게 아침은 차 한 잔으로 시작되어야 한다. 그렇지 않으면 그들은 그날의 남은 시간을 견뎌낼 수 없다! 그러므로 영국이 세계 최대의 차 소비국 중 하나인 것은 전혀 놀라운 일이 아니다. 이 나라에서는 하루에 다섯 잔은 평균에 불과하며 어떤 이들에게는 이 숫자가 거의 15잔에서 20

잔에 이른다. 실제로 제2차 세계 대전 중에, 윈스턴 처칠은 영국 병사들에게 차가 무기보다 더 중요하다고 말하기도 했다!

　영국의 차 관습은 중국과의 교역의 결과로 시작되었다. 중국에서 차를 마시는 전통은 기원전 3000년까지 거슬러 올라가지만, 영국에는 17세기 중반에서야 도래했다. 이 시기에 가장 일반적인 차는 녹차 종류였다. 하지만 19세기에는, 홍차가 선호하는 타입이 되었다. 영국의 차 문화가 형성되기 시작한 것도 이 무렵이었다. 다른 나라에서는 보통 아무것도 넣지 않고 차를 마셨지만 영국 사람들은 차에 우유와 설탕을 넣어 마시는 관습을 발달시켰다. 또한 하루 중 정해진 시간대나 특정한 경우에 차를 마셨다. '티 브레이크'나 '티타임', '티 파티' 같은 용어들은 이때 만들어진 것인데, 오늘날에도 일반적으로 사용된다.

　영국 사람들은 제대로 된 차를 만드는 일에도 정말 뛰어나다. 당신도 직접 쉽게 이것을 할 수 있다. 먼저, 마셔 보고 싶은 차 종류를 선택해라. 여기 몇 가지 인기 있는 선택지가 있다. 다르질링, 실론, 잉글리시 브렉퍼스트, 얼그레이가 그것이다. 물이 가득 담긴 찻주전자 안에 찻잎이 담긴 인퓨저를 넣는다. 편의를 위해 티백을 사용할 수도 있다. 물을 끓이고 그 후 몇 분간 그대로 둔다. 이제 차를 낼 준비가 되었으니, 기호에 따라 우유와 설탕을 넣으면 된다!

9행 **It** was also around this time **that** a British tea culture started to form.

▶ It ~ that ... 강조구문으로, 부사구인 around this time을 강조함

10행 British people developed a practice **of** drinking tea with milk and sugar, ...

▶ of는 '~라는'의 의미로 쓰여 동격을 나타냄

18행 **Place** an infuser [filled with loose tea] **into** a teapot [full of water].

▶ place A into B: A를 B에 넣다

READING 2   p. 44~45

WORD FOCUS   offer

provide 제공하다 / give 주다 / present 증정하다, 주다 / grant 수여하다, 주다

WORD CHECK

1. represent   2. lunar   3. taboo   4. compete
5. feast

▶ ancestor: a person whom one is descended from, and especially who lived a long time ago

정답

1. c   2. (1) F (2) T (3) F   3. Because she had to compete with other hungry ghosts for food.   4. d
5. b   6. b, d

해석

아시아의 일부 지역에서, 음력 7월은 유령의 달로 알려져 있다. 매년 유령의 달의 첫 번째 날에는 지옥의 문이 열린다고 한다. 이것은 유령들이 현실 세계로 돌아와 그달의 마지막 날에 지옥의 문이 다시 닫힐 때까지 머무를 수 있게 한다. 이 기간 동안, 사람들은 그들의 죽은 친척들을 기억하고 그들의 조상들에게 경의를 표한다.

유령의 달은 세 개의 중요한 날을 특징으로 한다. 첫 번째 날에는, 사람들이 옷과 돈을 상징하는 종이로 만든 작은 물건들을 태운다. 이것은 지옥에서 유령들에게 이 물건들을 제공한다고 믿어진다. 마지막 날에는, 사람들이 종이 등불을 강 위에 띄워 보낸다. 이 떠다니는 등불들은 유령들을 그들에게 제공된 물건들로 안내한다.

유령의 달의 가장 중요한 부분은 그달의 열다섯 번째 날에 기념하는 배고픈 유령 축제(중원절)이다. 그 축제 기간 동안, 배고픈 유령들에게 맛있는 진수성찬이 제공된다. 음식에 대한 보답으로, 유령들은 행운을 가져다준다. 한 전설에 따르면, 뮬리언이라는 이름의 남자가 지옥에 있는 그의 돌아가신 어머니를 걱정했다. 그녀는 음식을 두고 다른 배고픈 유령들과 경쟁해야만 했다. 그는 그녀에게 음식을 드리기 위해서 음력 7월 15일에 지옥으로 갔다. 많은 사람들은 이것이 축제 기간 동안 유령들에게 음식을 제공하는 전통으로 이어졌다고 생각한다.

유령의 달과 연관된 몇 가지 금기 사항이 있다. 사람들은 제물로 태워지는 종이 물건들을 밟아서는 안 된다. 밤 11시 이후에 빨간색이나 검은색 옷을 입는 것도 피해야 하는데, 왜냐하면 이러한 색깔들은 배고픈 유령들을 불러들일 수도 있기 때문이다. 마지막으로, 사람들은 그들의 옷을 말리기 위해 밖에 널어서는 안 되는데, 지나가는 유령들이 그것들을 훔쳐 갈 수도 있기 때문이다.

죽은 사람들을 기리는 것 외에도, 유령의 달은 사람들에게 올바른 행동에 대한 교훈을 준다. 조상들을 숭배하는 것은 가족 구성원에 대한 존경심을 갖게 하며, 유령들에게 제물을 바치는 것은 나눔의 중요성을 나타낸다.

구문 해설

4행 This **allows** ghosts **to return** to the world of the living and **(to) stay** until the gates of Hell close again on the last day of the month.
▶ allow + 목적어 + to-v: ~이 …하도록 해 주다

9행 On the first day, people burn small items [**made** of paper], [**representing** clothes and money].
▶ 과거분사구 made of paper와 현재분사구 representing 이하가 동시에 small items를 수식

11행 These floating lanterns guide the ghosts to the items [**being offered** to them].

▶ being 이하는 the items를 수식하며 being은 생략 가능

23행 **In addition to** honoring *the dead*, the Ghost Month gives people a lesson about proper behaviors.
▶ in addition to: ~에 더하여, ~일 뿐 아니라
▶ the + 형용사: ~인 사람들 (복수보통명사)

WORD REVIEW TEST

UNIT 07   p. 46

1. a   2. b   3. d   4. b   5. c   6. a   7. c   8. c
9. a   10. d   11. efficiency   12. confuse
13. population   14. sustainable

UNIT 08   p. 47

1. d   2. a   3. c   4. b   5. c   6. d   7. a   8. b
9. weapons   10. represent   11. competing
12. encourage   13. celebrate   14. form   15. term
16. attract

UNIT 09.
Origins

READING 1   p. 48~49

WORD FOCUS   enemy

rival 경쟁자 / foe 적 / opponent (게임 · 대회 등의) 상대 / competitor 경쟁 상대

WORD CHECK

1. checkered   2. kingdom   3. resemble   4. wheat
5. reward

▶ capture: to move into a square occupied by an opponent's piece and remove it from the chessboard

정답

1. c   2. Because a powerful king ordered him to invent an exciting game for him.   3. b   4. d   5. d
6. invent, armies, reward, double, spread

　　두 선수가 침묵 속에 서로를 응시한다. 갑자기, 한 선수가 말을 움직인다. 그는 다른 선수의 왕을 잡고 게임에서 승리한다! 이 게임은 체스로, 그 역사가 수 세기에 이른다. 그것은 (가로·세로) 8×8의 격자형으로 배열된 정사각형의 체크무늬 보드 위에서 이루어진다.

　　당신은 전에 체스를 둬 봤을지도 모르지만, 그것이 어디서 유래했는지 아는가? 체스의 최초 버전은 6세기 인도에서 등장했다. 설화에 따르면, 강한 권력을 가진 왕이 가난한 수학자에게 자신을 위해 흥미로운 게임을 고안하라고 명령했다. 그 수학자는 각각 한 명의 왕에 의해 통솔되는 두 개의 군대가 있는 게임을 만들어 냈다. 그 게임의 말은 보병, 기마병, 코끼리와 전차를 포함했는데, 이것들 모두 64개의 정사각형으로 된 보드 위에 놓여 있었다. 목표는 상대편의 왕을 잡는 것이었다.

　　왕은 그 게임을 매우 마음에 들어 했고, 수학자에게 보상을 약속했다. 그 수학자는 영리하게도 보드의 첫 번째 정사각형에 한 개의 밀 낟알을 놓고, 왕에게 보드의 나머지 각 정사각형마다 그 밀알을 두 배씩 늘리도록 요청했다. 처음에 왕은 그것이 그다지 많아 보이지 않는다고 여겼다. 그는 자기 신하들에게 밀알을 세기 시작하라고 명령했다. 밀알의 숫자가 계속 두 배씩 늘어나자, 밀 더미는 거대해졌다. 결국, 왕은 왕국 전체에도 충분한 밀알이 없다는 것을 깨달았다. 웃으면서, 왕은 수학자가 천재임을 인정했다.

　　수 세기에 걸쳐, 그 게임은 인도 전역에서 대중화되었고 서양으로 전파되기 시작했다. 한때 유럽에서 그 게임 말들은 유럽 스타일로 발전하기 시작했다. 예를 들어, 기마병과 전차 대신에 나이트(기사)와 룩(성)이 있었다. 15세기에 이르자, 그 게임은 현대판 체스를 닮아 가기 시작했다. 그것은 한때 인도의 한 왕을 위한 게임이었지만, 지금은 전 세계 사람들에 의해 행해진다.

구문 해설

5행 It is played on a checkered board, **with** squares **arranged** on an 8×8 grid.
▶ with + 목적어 + p.p.: ~이 …된 상태인

7행 ..., but do you know [**where** it comes from]?
▶ where 이하는 간접의문문으로 「의문사 + 주어 + 동사」의 어순

10행 The mathematician created a game with two armies, [each led by a king].

13행 The king loved the game and **promised** the mathematician a reward.
　　　　　　　　　　　　　　　　　　IO　　　　DO
▶ promise + 간접목적어 + 직접목적어: ~에게 …을 약속하다

19행 **Laughing**, he recognized that the mathematician was a genius.
▶ Laughing은 동시동작을 나타내는 분사구문

WORD FOCUS　bomb

a fake bomb 가짜 폭탄 / drop a bomb 폭탄을 투하하다 / a bomb threat 폭파 위협

WORD CHECK

1. declare　2. harsh　3. arrest　4. sympathetic
5. firework
▶ bonfire: a big outdoor fire used for burning things or celebrating

정답

1. c　2. He treated them[Catholics] very badly.
3. c　4. d　5. (1) T (2) F　6. celebrate, failed, model, bonfire, fireworks

해석

　　만일 가이 포크스의 계획이 성공했더라면 우리는 그를 세계 최초의 유명 테러리스트로 기억하고 있을지도 모른다. 대신에 매년 11월 5일, 영국 사람들은 그의 모형들을 만든다. 그리고 밤이 되면 그 모형들을 불 위에 올려놓고 태운다.

　　가이 포크스는 무엇을 하려고 했던 것일까? 1605년 제임스 1세는 영국의 왕이었다. 그는 가톨릭교도들을 매우 혹독하게 대했다. 그런 혹독한 처우에 지쳐서, 가이 포크스와 다른 7명의 가톨릭교도들은 제임스 왕과 영국 정부의 모든 관계자를 살해하려는 계획을 세웠다. 그들은 국회 의사당 지하에 거대한 폭탄을 숨겨 두었다. 가이 포크스는 제임스 왕과 정부 관리 모두가 11월 5일 밤에 그곳에 있으리라는 것을 알고 있었다. 하지만 폭탄을 점화시키려고 갔을 때, 왕실 근위대가 그를 발견하고 체포했다.

　　그가 체포된 직후에, 영국 정부는 11월 5일을 기념일로 선포하였다. 400년이 넘은 지금은 가이 포크스라는 사람 자체는 간혹 좀 더 동정적으로 기억되기도 하지만, '가이 포크스 데이'는 여전히 기념되고 있다. 사람들은 그 중요한 날 밤을 위한 준비를 하며 몇 주를 보낸다. 상점들은 폭죽 상자를 팔기 시작하고, 사람들은 그들이 가장 좋아하는 종류를 산다. 모든 사람이 모닥불을 피우기 위해 나무, 나뭇잎, 정원의 쓰레기를 모은다.

　　전통적으로, 아이들은 '가이'라고 불리는 가이 포크스 모형들을 들고, "가이에게 한 푼만요!"라고 외치며 길거리를 다닌다. 그것이 괜찮은 모형이라고 생각하면 사람들은 그 아이들에게 돈을 조금 줄 것이다. 그러면 아이들은 그 돈을 폭죽을 사는 데 쓴다.

　　11월 5일 밤이 되면 사람들은 그들의 정원에서 불꽃놀이를 한다. 그런 다음 모닥불 주위에 빙 둘러서서 전통적인 가이 포크스 데이 음식인 소시지와 감자를 요리한다. 당연히 마지막으로 사람들은 그가 저지르려 했던 범죄를 생각하면서 '가이'를 모닥불 위에 올려놓고 태운다.

구문 해설

1행 If Guy Fawkes's plan **had succeeded**, we **might remember** him as the world's ....
▶ 종속절이 가정법 과거완료, 주절이 가정법 과거인 혼합 가정법

15

(Being) Tired of the harsh treatment, Guy Fawkes and seven other Catholics made <u>a plan</u> *to kill* King

James ....

▶ (Being) Tired ... treatment는 이유를 나타내는 분사구문 (= As they were tired of ...)

▶ to kill 이하는 a plan을 수식하는 형용사적 용법의 to부정사

16행 People **spend** several weeks *getting* ready for the big night.

▶ spend + 시간 + v-ing: ~을 하면서 시간을 보내다

▶ get ready for: ~에 대비하다

20행 Traditionally, children take their models ... through the streets, **shouting** "A penny for the guy!"

▶ shouting 이하는 동시동작을 나타내는 분사구문

22행 The children then **spend** the money **on** fireworks.

▶ spend + 돈 + on ~: ~에 돈을 쓰다

UNIT 10.
Geology

READING 1   p. 52~53

WORD FOCUS   reason

a main reason 주요 이유 / a simple reason 단순한 이유 / have (a) reason 이유가 있다 / give a reason 이유를 들다[제시하다]

WORD CHECK

1. faraway   2. severe   3. deposit   4. insight
5. emblem

▶ abundance: a very large amount of sth

정답

1. c   2. a   3. They first increased and then decreased.
4. b   5. c   6. (1) ⓑ (2) ⓒ (3) ⓐ

해석

　　호주는 오팔의 땅이다. 이 귀한 원석이 그 나라의 국가적 상징인 데는 충분한 이유가 있다. 전 세계 오팔의 90퍼센트 이상이, 때론 '레드 센터'라고 불리는 호주의 외딴 중앙 지역에서 나오기 때문이다. 그것들은 퀸즐랜드주, 사우스오스트레일리아주, 뉴사우스웨일스주의 사막 지역에서 혹독한 기후 조건 속에 채굴된다. 오팔의 풍부한 매장량과 인기에도 불구하고, 과학자들은 최근까지 어떻게, 왜 지구상의 오팔 중 그렇게 많은 양이 호주에서 형성되었는지를 정확히 설명할 수 없었다.

　　시드니 대학의 최근 연구 결과는 오팔의 불가사의한 형성 과정에 새로운 통찰을 제공해 주었다. 약 1억 년 전, 호주의 60퍼센트를 뒤덮고 있던 내륙해가 마르기 시작했다. 이는 그 지역의 암석, 토양, 광물질 구성에 놀라운 변화를 일으켰다. 바다의 산성도가 처음에는 높아졌다가 그 다음엔 낮아졌다. 이는 오팔이 형성되기 위한 최적의 조건을 만드는 데 일조했다. 중앙 오스트레일리아는 이런 식의 변화가 그토록 대규모로 일어난 지구상의 유일한 장소로 알려져 있다.

　　놀랍게도, 이런 발견들은 우리가 화성의 환경을 더 잘 이해하는 데 도움이 될지도 모른다. 중앙 오스트레일리아의 적색토와 지형은 그 붉은 행성(화성)의 표면과 많은 특징을 공유하고 있다. 2008년에 우주 비행사들은 그 행성에서 오팔과 유사한 매장 층을 발견했고, 이는 오팔이 그곳에도 존재할지 모른다는 믿음에 힘을 실어 주었다. 화성에서의 오팔의 발견은 화성과 중앙 오스트레일리아의 지형 사이의 유사점을 한층 더 입증하는 열쇠가 될 수 있다. 이것은 과학자들이 바로 여기 지구에서, 멀리 떨어진 행성에 혹시 존재할 수도 있는 생물학적인 과정을 연구할 수 있을지도 모른다는 것을 의미한다.

구문 해설

8행   ..., scientists **were unable** until recently **to explain** exactly [*how* or *why* so many of the earth's opals formed in Australia].

▶ be unable to-v: ~할 수 없다

▶ how와 why가 이끄는 절은 explain의 목적어로 쓰인 간접의문문으로 「의문사 + 주어 + 동사」의 어순

15행   Central Australia is known to be <u>the only place on</u> <u>earth</u> [where these types of changes have ever occurred on **such a large scale**].

▶ such a(n) + 형용사 + 명사: 그렇게 ~한 …

20행   ..., **strengthening** <u>the belief</u> *that* opals may also exist there.

▶ strengthening 이하는 부대상황을 나타내는 분사구문

▶ that이 이끄는 절은 the belief와 동격 관계

READING 2   TOEFL   p. 54~55

정답

1. d   2. the fourth square   3. c   4. c   5. c
6. c, d, e

해석

샌안드레아스 단층

　　태평양판과 북아메리카판 사이의 경계 부분인 샌안드레아스 단층은 캘리포니아주 북부 해안을 따라 지나고 있고 주의 남부 지역의 내륙으로 뻗어 있다. 그것은 1895년에 발견되었고 샌안드레아스 호수의 이름을 따서 지어졌는데 그 호수는 이 판들의 이동으로 형성되었다.

이 (판들의) 이동은 여러모로 캘리포니아의 지형 형성도 도왔다. 그것들은 아름다운 산과 계곡을 만들었다. 하지만 샌안드레아스 단층은 심각한 우려도 낳고 있다. 그 판들은 오늘날에도 여전히 움직이고 있어서 그 지역의 지대를 위험할 만큼 불안정하게 만들고 있다.

샌안드레아스 단층은 변환 단층이다. 이는 그것을 형성하는 판들이 서로를 지나쳐 움직이고 있다는 것을 의미한다. 그것들이 반대 방향으로 움직이고 있기 때문에 심각한 지진이 일어날 가능성이 높다. 그 단층이 여러 인구 밀집 지역을 지나가기 때문에 특히 걱정거리가 되고 있다. 실제로 1906년 샌프란시스코에 대규모 지진이 발생했다. 그것은 도시의 상당 부분을 파괴했으며 이러한 판의 이동들이 얼마나 파괴적일 수 있는지 보여 주었다.

지진은 예측하기 매우 어렵지만 판 경계를 좀 더 주의 깊게 연구하는 것은 과학자들이 이러한 자연재해에 대비해 더 나은 경보 체계를 개발하는 데 도움이 될 수 있다. 육지에 있는 보기 드문 판 경계 중 하나인 샌안드레아스 단층은 다른 판 경계보다 연구하기에 훨씬 더 쉬운데, 다른 판 경계들은 대개 해저에서 발견되기 때문이다. 지질학자들은 그것을 자세히 연구하고, 다음 대지진이 언제 일어날지 예측하는 데 도움이 될 수 있는 징후들을 주의 깊게 관찰하고 있다.

구문 해설

3행 It was discovered in 1895 and (**was**) **named after** San Andreas Lake, *which* was formed by the movements of these plates.
▶ be named after: ~의 이름을 따서 명명되다
▶ which는 San Andreas Lake를 선행사로 하는 계속적 용법의 관계대명사

7행 The plates are still moving today, and they **make** the ground in the area dangerously **unstable**.
▶ make + 목적어 + 형용사: ~을 …하게 만들다

10행 ..., there is a high chance **of** *serious earthquakes* **occurring**.
▶ of는 '~라는'의 의미로 쓰여 동격을 나타냄
▶ serious earthquakes는 동명사 occurring의 의미상의 주어

16행 ..., is **much** easier *to study* than other plate boundaries, ...
▶ much: 훨씬 (비교급 강조)
▶ to study는 easier를 수식하는 부사적 용법의 to부정사

WORD REVIEW TEST

p. 56

1. c   2. a   3. d   4. a   5. c   6. b   7. a   8. b
9. d   10. c   11. a   12. grain   13. arrange
14. modern

---

p. 57

1. d   2. b   3. c   4. a   5. c   6. a   7. b   8. d   9. a
10. c   11. unstable   12. mine   13. precious
14. landscape

UNIT 11.
Space

READING 1   p. 58~59

WORD FOCUS   trip

journey 여행, 여정 / voyage 여행, (우주·바다로의) 항해 / expedition 탐험, 원정 / tour 여행, 관광

WORD CHECK

1. destination   2. crater   3. range   4. spacesuit
5. bounce
▶ pressure: a force pushing on sb or sth

정답

1. d   2. c   3. The pressure of the atmosphere there is 90 times greater than it is on Earth.   4. a   5. extreme, freezing, atmosphere, crushed, adjust

해석

우리 대부분은 우주여행이 우리 생애에 가능해지기를 희망한다. 잠시 그것을 상상해 보아라. 당신은 개인 우주선에 뛰어올라 타고 화성에서의 하이킹이나 은하계를 통과하는 별 관측 여행을 위해 출발한다. 당신은 무엇을 가져가야 할까? 분명, 당신은 카메라와 여행을 위한 맛있는 간식이 좀 필요할 것이다. 그러나 무엇보다도, 알맞은 종류의 우주복을 입어야 한다는 것을 기억하라. 그것 없이는 지구에서 가장 가까운 몇몇 목적지에서 살아남을 수 없을 것이다.

수성부터 시작하자. 그곳은 깊은 분화구들과 높은 절벽들이 있는, 탐사하기에 재미있는 행성이다. 그러나 수성에는 공기가 없어서 당신은 반드시 산소가 충분한 우주복이 필요하다. 또한, 기온 차가 섭씨 영하 173도에서 영상 427도에 이르니, 당신이 꽁꽁 얼거나 타 버리는 것을 막아 주는 우주복을 입어라.

다음은 금성이다. 솔직히, 금성은 아주 좋은 휴가지는 아니다. 그곳은 너무 더운 데다 날씨가 흐리며, 그곳의 대기는 대부분 이산화탄소이다. 게다가, 그곳의 기압은 지구 기압보다 90배나 높다. 따라서 당신을 보호해 줄 티타늄 우주복이 필요하다. 티타늄 우주복이 없다면, 당신은 즉시 으스러질 것이다.

가장 안전한 목적지는 확실히 달이다. 달의 중력은 지구 중력의 약 1/6 정도의 세기이다. 그래서 당신은 쉽게 주변을 뛰어다니며 탐사할 수

있다. 무엇보다, 대부분의 우주복이 여기에서 잘 작동한다. 그러나 당신의 우주복에 반드시 온도 제어 장치를 달아라. 달에서는 기온 차가 섭씨 영하 173도에서 영상 100도에 이른다. 그리고 그곳에는 공기가 없으므로 산소가 필요할 것이다. 그러나 당신에게 어떤 문제가 생기더라도, 근처에 바로 이용 가능한 달 기지가 있을 것이다!

구문 해설

11행 Also, temperatures **range from** -173°C **to** 427°C, so wear a spacesuit that *prevents* you *from freezing* or *burning*.
▶ range from A to B: 범위가 A에서 B에 이르다
▶ prevent + 목적어 + from v-ing: ~이 …하는 것을 막다

14행 In addition, the pressure of the atmosphere there is **90 times greater than** it is on Earth.
(= 90 times as great as)
▶ 배수사 + 비교급 + than ~: ~보다 … 배 ~한 (= 배수사 + as + 원급 + as ~)

17행 Gravity on the moon is around 1/6th as strong as **that** of Earth.
▶ that은 앞에 언급된 Gravity를 가리킴

24행 ..., there **should** be a handy moon base nearby!
▶ 조동사 should는 '~일 것이다'라는 뜻으로, 근거 있는 추측을 나타냄

READING 2
p. 60~61

WORD FOCUS bath

take a bath 목욕하다 / a warm bath 따뜻한 (물에 하는) 목욕 / bath water 목욕물 / bath time 목욕 시간

WORD CHECK

1. regular 2. conserve 3. strap 4. suffer from
5. pastime
▶ float: to move softly upon or through the water or the air

정답

1. c 2. d 3. Because human muscle and bone weaken in space. 4. d 5. (1) conserved (2) straw (3) strapped (4) weakens (5) bar

해석

당신은 아마도 우주에 있는 우주 비행사들의 사진을 본 적이 있을 것이다. 그들이 둥둥 떠다니면서 무중력의 느낌을 즐기고 있는 모습을 말이다. 하지만 우주에 사는 것이 늘 재미있고 즐겁기만 할까? 우주 비행사의 평상시 하루는 어떤 모습일까?

사실 국제 우주 정거장에는 '하루'라는 게 없다. 이 정거장은 지구 주위를 너무 빠르게 돌아서 해가 24시간마다 15번씩 뜬다. 하지만 우주 비행

사들은 본래의 24시간 생체 시계에 맞춰 일하고 자야 하는데, 그렇게 하지 않으면 얼마 안 있어 끊임없는 시차증을 겪게 된다. 따라서 우주 비행사들은 때맞춰 그들을 깨워줄 자명종을 사용한다.

잠에서 깨면, 씻을 차례이다. 하지만 샤워를 하는 대신, 우주 비행사들은 스펀지 목욕을 한다. 이는 물을 아래로 끌어당기는 중력이 없으면 물이 몸에 붙어 있기 때문이다. 그것은 또한 물을 절약해 주기도 하는데, 우주 정거장에서는 물의 공급량이 한정적이다.

그다음으로 우주 비행사들은 옷을 입고 아침 식사를 위해 자리에 앉는다. 우주 음식은 대개 비닐봉지에 들어 있고 빨대로 마셔야 한다. 그렇지 않으면 음식이 주변에 둥둥 떠다닐 것이다. 우주 비행사들도 이따금 보통 음식을 먹긴 하지만 음식은 끈으로 접시에 고정되어 있고, 접시, 칼, 그리고 포크에는 자석이 달려 있다.

우주 비행사들은 많은 과학적인 업무로 온종일 바쁘지만 운동도 반드시 해야 한다. 인간의 근육과 뼈는 우주에서 약해지므로, 우주 비행사들이 건강을 유지할 수 있도록 실내 운동용 자전거가 있다. 그리고 이 밖에도 우주 비행사들은 매일 무엇을 해야 할까? 그렇다, 화장실은 어떨까? 우주에서는 화장실에서 물을 사용하지 않는다. 강력한 봉이 우주 비행사들을 자리에 고정해 주고, 송풍기가 진공청소기처럼 변기를 비워 준다.

하루가 끝나갈 무렵이 되면, 우주 비행사들은 침낭을 벽에 고정하고 잠잘 준비를 한다. 아니면 그들은 창문 하나를 찾아 우주에서 가장 인기 있는 취미를 즐길 수도 있다. 수백 킬로미터 아래에서 세상이 돌아가는 모습을 바라보는 것 말이다.

구문 해설

7행 The station speeds around Earth **so** quickly **that** the sun rises 15 times every 24 hours.
▶ so ~ that ...: 너무 ~하여 …하다 (결과)

16행 ..., and the dishes, knives, and forks have magnets attached.

24행 ... the most popular pastime in space—*watching* the world *go* by hundreds of kilometers below.
▶ watching 이하는 the most popular pastime in space와 동격 관계
▶ watch(지각동사) + 목적어 + 동사원형: ~이 …하는 것을 보다

UNIT 12.
Technology

READING 1
p. 62~63

WORD FOCUS speed

an average speed 평균 속도 / at full speed 전속력으로 / reduce the speed 속도를 줄이다 / speed limit 제한 속도

WORD CHECK

1. measure   2. lifelike   3. crash   4. alter   5. sensor
▶ alternative: one of two or more options to replace sth

정답

1. b   2. c   3. d   4. It shows whether a crash would cause injuries that could lead to death.   5. c   6. (1) ⓐ (2) ⓓ (3) ⓒ (4) ⓑ

해석

수십 년 전에는 사람들이 심각한 자동차 사고에서 거의 살아남지 못했다. 오늘날의 자동차들은 안전성 검사의 개선 덕분에 훨씬 더 안전하다. 자동차 안전성 검사 동안 새 자동차는 빠른 속도로 벽에 충돌하게 된다. 자동차 안에는 '충돌 실험용 인형'이라고 불리는 승객 크기의 인형이 있다. 이 충돌 실험용 인형을 연구함으로써 과학자들은 충돌 시 실제 승객들에게 어떤 일이 일어날지를 알 수 있고 자동차의 안전성을 개선할 수 있게 된다.

오늘날의 충돌 실험용 인형들은 가능한 한 인간과 흡사하게 만들어진다. 인형의 인공 피부 안쪽에는 우리처럼 갈비뼈가 있다. 그것들은 심지어 쇠와 고무로 만들어진 척추도 갖고 있다. 인형의 무릎과 발목은 사고 시 사람의 것과 똑같이 움직이도록 설계되어 있다. 그것들은 또한 다양한 크기로 제작되며, 더 작은 '여성'과 한층 더 작은 '어린이' 인형을 포함한 충돌 실험용 인형 가족이 있다.

충돌 실험용 인형에는 충돌의 충격을 측정하는 세 가지 다른 종류의 감지기가 있다. 머리, 다리 및 기타 부위의 감지기는 충돌 시 신체 부위가 얼마나 빨리 움직이는지를 보여 준다. 또 다른 감지기는 우리의 뼈가 부러지기 전에 얼마나 많은 압력을 견딜 수 있는지를 기록한다. 마지막으로 가슴 부위 안에 있는 감지기는 충돌이 사망으로 이어질 수 있는 부상을 유발하는지를 보여 준다.

충돌 실험용 인형은 매우 첨단 기술인데, 몹시 비싸기도 하다. 한 개 가격이 무려 10만 달러 이상이다. 하지만 더욱 저렴한 대안이 개발되는 중이다. '가상' 충돌 실험용 인형은 오직 컴퓨터 화면에서만 존재하지만, 오늘날의 충돌 실험용 인형보다 훨씬 더 실제 같이 만드는 것이 가능할지도 모른다. 가상 인형은 어떠한 키나 몸무게를 가진 사람이라도 닮게끔 쉽게 바뀔 수 있으며, 무엇보다도 그것들은 손상 없이 몇 번이고 사용될 수 있다. 미래에는 이 가상 인형이 충돌 실험이 시행되는 방식을 완전히 바꿀지도 모른다.

구문 해설

8행 Today's crash test dummies are built to **be** *as* much **like** human beings *as possible*.
▶ be like: ~와 같다, ~와 유사하다
▶ as ~ as possible: 가능한 한 ~한[하게]

10행 Their knees and ankles are designed to act just like ours **do** in accidents.
(= our knees and ankles)
▶ do는 반복을 피하기 위해 동사 act를 대신해 쓰인 대동사

16행 ... **whether** a crash would cause injuries [that could lead to death].

▶ whether: ~인지 아닌지

23행 ..., **best of all**, they can be used over and over *without being* damaged.
▶ best of all: 무엇보다도
▶ without v-ing: ~하지 않고

READING 2   p. 64~65

WORD FOCUS   steady

unstable 불안정한 / vulnerable 취약한, 연약한 / unfixed 고정되지 않은

WORD CHECK

1. transparent   2. glue   3. thigh   4. model
5. innovation
▶ microscopic: tiny and unable to be seen by the naked eye

정답

1. c   2. It is designed to bear the weight of a standing human being.   3. (1) ⓒ (2) ⓐ (3) ⓑ   4. c   5. b
6. design, bear, inspired, modeled, solutions

해석

파리의 에펠탑은 지금까지 인간이 창조한 가장 유명한 건축물들 중 하나이다. 그러나 탑 설계 이면의 발상에 대해서 아는 사람은 많지 않다. 사실, 에펠탑은 인간의 대퇴골(넓적다리뼈)을 본떠 만든 것이다!

1850년대에 대퇴골에 대한 흥미로운 발견이 이루어졌다. 해부학자들은 골두(뼈끝)라고 불리는, 대퇴골 상단부를 연구하던 중이었는데, 그것은 고관절(넓적다리관절)과 연결되는 부위이다. 대퇴골 골두는 서 있는 인간의 체중을 지탱하기 위해 특수하게 설계되어 있다. 그것의 내부 구조는 마치 우리에 있는 창살처럼 서로 연결된 다수의 작은 버팀보들로 이루어져 있다. 이러한 흥미로운 구조가 대퇴골이 체중을 지탱할 수 있게 하는 것이다. 공학자인 구스타브 에펠은 대퇴골의 구조가 매우 인상적이라고 여겨, 이를 에펠탑을 설계하는 데 이용했다. 이 구조가 강풍에서도 탑이 안정을 유지할 수 있는 이유이다.

에펠탑 외에도, 자연을 본뜬 다른 인공 건축물들을 세계 여러 곳에서 찾아볼 수 있다. 예를 들어, 뮌헨의 올림픽 경기장 지붕은 잠자리 날개의 디자인에 기초한 것이다. 그것은 수천 개의 작은 투명한 부분들로 이루어져 있어, 견고함을 부여할 뿐만 아니라 빛도 통과시킨다. 그리고 접착제보다 더 강하지만 쉽게 붙였다 떼었다 할 수 있는 게코 테이프는 게코 도마뱀의 발가락에 있는 미세 섬모를 본떠서 만들어졌다.

이것들을 비롯한 기타 혁신적인 것들은 실은 우리가 자연에서 배울 것이 많다는 것을 보여 준다. 사람들은 우리가 직면하는 문제 중 많은 것들에 대한 해결책이 자연계에 이미 존재하고 있을지도 모른다는 것을 깨닫기 시작하고 있다. 우리가 해야 할 일은 그것들을 찾는 것뿐이다.

| 7행 | Anatomists were studying the top of the thigh bone, called the head, **which** connects to the hip joint. |

▶ which는 the top of the thigh bone을 선행사로 하는 계속적 용법의 관계대명사 (= and it)

| 10행 | This interesting structure is **what** *enables* the thigh bone *to support* the body's weight. |
(S V C)

▶ what은 선행사를 포함한 관계대명사

▶ enable + 목적어 + to-v: ∼이 …할 수 있게 하다

| 13행 | This structure is (the reason) **why** the tower can remain steady in strong winds. |

▶ 관계부사 why 앞에는 선행사 the reason이 생략됨

| 24행 | All (**that**) we have to do is (*to*) find them. |

▶ All 뒤에 목적격 관계대명사 that이 생략됨

▶ All ∼ is[was] … 구문에서 be동사 뒤에 보어로 쓰인 to부정사의 to는 보통 생략됨

WORD REVIEW TEST

UNIT 11
p. 66

1. b 2. d 3. d 4. c 5. a 6. c 7. b 8. floating
9. attached 10. weaken 11. instantly
12. atmosphere 13. crush 14. gravity 15. magnet

UNIT 12
p. 67

1. b 2. a 3. d 4. b 5. b 6. c 7. a
8. resemble 9. measure 10. modeled
11. impact 12. virtual 13. passenger 14. joint
15. pressure

UNIT 13.
Health

READING 1
p. 68~69

WORD FOCUS effect

major effect 큰 영향[효과] / negative effect 부정적인 영향[효과] / long-term effect 장기적인 영향[효과] / have an effect (on) (∼에) 영향을 미치다

WORD CHECK

1. fake 2. subject 3. phenomenon 4. numerous
5. disorder

▶ shot: an injection of a substance into the body through a needle

정답

1. d 2. They quit the study because of dizziness and nausea. 3. b 4. (1) F (2) T (3) T 5. opposite, expectations, possible, dishonest

해석

플라세보 효과는 잘 알려진 현상이다. 환자들은 가짜 약이 그들에게 도움이 될 것이라는 기대로 인해 가짜 약으로부터 긍정적인 효과를 얻을 수 있다. 그러나 이것은 또한 정반대로도 작용할 수 있다. 덜 흔하게 논의되지만 이러한 상황은 노시보 효과라고 불린다.

다수의 연구에 따르면, 상당수 환자가 불쾌한 부작용 때문에 그들에게 처방된 가짜 약의 복용을 중단한다. 예를 들어, 만성 통증 질환 약을 시험할 때, 연구원들은 일부 피실험자들에게 가짜 약을 투여했다. 그들은 이 사람들의 11%가 어지러움과 메스꺼움 때문에 실험 참가를 (중도에) 포기했음을 알게 되었다. 그 피실험자들은 이러한 부작용들이 나타날 거라고 예상해서 자신들이 정말 그것들을 겪고 있는 것처럼 느꼈다.

노시보 효과는 환자들이 진짜 약을 복용할 때도 일어날 수 있다. 의사가 환자에게 발생 가능한 약의 부작용들에 대해 말해 줄 때 환자는 그것들을 경험할 가능성이 더 높다. 심지어 의사가 사용하는 특정한 말도 노시보 효과를 일으킬 수 있다. 예를 들어, 분만 중인 여성들은 종종 고통을 줄이기 위해 주사를 맞는다. 한 실험에서 일부 여성들은 주사를 맞으면 한결 나아질 거라는 말을 들었다. 나머지 여성들은 주사 자체가 아플 것이라는 말을 들었다. 의사가 선택한 말 때문에 후자 그룹은 전자 그룹보다 주사가 더 아팠다고 전했다.

노시보 효과 때문에 의사들은 어려운 결정에 직면한다. 한편으로, 그들은 그들의 환자에게 전적으로 솔직해지길 원한다. 그러나 다른 한편으로, 그들은 그들의 환자가 불필요한 고통이나 부작용을 겪게 되길 원하지 않는다. 전문가들은 가장 좋은 해결책은 의사들이 그들의 환자와 명확히 의사소통하되 부정적인 것들을 강조하지 않는 것이라고 생각한다.

구문 해설

| 1행 | Patients can receive positive effects … due to their expectation that it will help them. |
(their =)

| 5행 | …, a significant **number of patients** *stop taking* the fake medicine [given to them] because of unpleasant side effects. |

▶ a number of + 복수명사: 많은 ∼

▶ stop v-ing: ∼하는 것을 멈추다

| 9행 | Those subjects **expected** these side effects **to occur**, so they truly felt *as though* they were **suffering from** them. |

▶ expect + 목적어 + to-v: ~이 …할 것으로 예상[기대]하다

▶ as though: 마치 ~인 것처럼 (= as if)

▶ suffer from: ~을 겪대[앓다]

(16행) ..., the latter group reported the shot to be more
S V O OC
painful than the former group did.
(= reported)

(20행) Experts believe [**that** the best solution is *for doctors* **to communicate** clearly with their patients, but **to avoid** emphasizing negative things].

▶ that 이하는 동사 believe의 목적어 역할

▶ for doctors는 to부정사인 to communicate와 to avoid의 의미상의 주어

READING 2   p. 70~71

WORD FOCUS common

rare 드문, 희귀한 / unusual 특이한, 드문 / exceptional 보통이 아닌, 드문

WORD CHECK

1. resistance   2. respiratory   3. infection   4. adapt
5. reproduce

▶ sneeze: to suddenly blow air out through the nose

정답

1. c   2. Because it is the key to proper treatment.
3. (1) T (2) T (3) F   4. b   5. Causes, bigger, multiply,
kill, regularly

해석

　재채기하기, 기침하기, 그리고 콧물 처리하기는 매우 불편할 수 있다! 다행히도, 이러한 증상과 연관된 감기나 다른 감염병은 건강한 성인에게는 대개 심각하지 않다. 그러나 감염의 원인이 박테리아인지 혹은 바이러스인지를 아는 것은 중요한데, 그것이 적절한 치료의 열쇠이기 때문이다.

　박테리아는 귀, 폐, 기도, 목의 감염과 같은 일부 질환의 원인이 된다. 그러나 보통의 감기와 독감을 포함한 대부분의 호흡기 감염병은 바이러스에 의해 유발된다. 박테리아와 바이러스는 매우 다르다. 박테리아는 증식하기 위해 분열하는 단세포 생물이다. 한편, 바이러스는 훨씬 더 작고 혼자서는 살아남거나 증식할 수 없다. 그것들은 세포를 장악하여 그것들을 이용해 번식함으로써 퍼져 나간다.

　박테리아와 바이러스의 가장 중요한 차이점 가운데 하나는 그것들이 치료되는 방식이다. 일단 의사들이 감염병의 원인을 찾기 위한 검사를 하면, 그들은 환자들에게 어떤 종류의 약을 처방해야 하는지 알 수 있다. 항생제는 박테리아를 죽이지만 바이러스를 퇴치하지는 못한다. 바이러스가 세포를 장악해 번식하는 것을 막는 데는 다른 종류의 약이 필요하다. 불필요할 때 환자들에게 항생제를 처방하는 것은 위험을 초래할 수 있다. 이는 박테리아가 항생제에 더 많이 노출될수록 그것들은 항생제에 더 적응하여 그에 대

한 저항력을 기를 수 있기 때문이다. 항생제가 특정 박테리아에 작용하지 않게 되면, 그 박테리아에 의해 생긴 감염병을 치료하기 훨씬 더 어려워진다.

　당연히 애초에 호흡기 감염병에 걸리지 않도록 하는 것이 최선이다. 바이러스는 누군가가 재채기나 기침을 한 뒤 얼마간 공기 중에 살아남을 수 있기 때문에 특히 쉽게 퍼진다. 그것들은 문손잡이와 같이 함께 쓰는 물건에 퍼질 수도 있다. 그것이 잦은 손 씻기가 매우 중요한 이유이다.

구문 해설

(2행) Luckily, having a cold or other infection [**that** is
S
linked to these symptoms] generally isn't serious ....
V

▶ that은 a cold or other infection을 선행사로 하는 주격 관계대명사

(5행) However, **it** is important **to know** [*whether* the cause of the infection is bacteria *or* a virus], ...

▶ it은 가주어, to know 이하가 진주어

▶ whether A or B: A인지 B인지

(11행) Meanwhile, viruses are **much** smaller and cannot survive or multiply *on their own*.

▶ much: 훨씬 (비교급 강조)

▶ on one's own: 스스로, 혼자서

(12행) They spread *by* **taking** over cells and **using** them to reproduce.

▶ taking, using은 전치사 by의 목적어로 쓰인 동명사로 이 둘은 병렬관계임

(19행) This is because **the more** bacteria are exposed to antibiotics, **the more** they are able to adapt and (to) build up a resistance to them.

▶ the + 비교급 ~, the + 비교급 ...: 더 ~할수록 더 …하다

UNIT 14.
Psychology

READING 1   p. 72~73

WORD FOCUS discover

find out (조사하여) 발견하다, 생각해 내다 / learn ~을 알게 되다 / realize 깨닫다, 알아차리다

WORD CHECK

1. partial   2. recall   3. state   4. syllable   5. activate

▶ cue: a signal to do sth

1. a   2. a, c   3. d   4. It refers to struggling but then retrieving a memory.   5. d   6. (1) ⓓ (2) ⓐ (3) ⓑ (4) ⓒ

해석

당신은 어떤 질문에 대한 답을 알고 있지만, 어떤 까닭인지 적합한 단어를 떠올릴 수 없는 것을 느껴본 적이 있는가? 이 상태는 '적확언어망각,' 즉 '설단' 현상으로 알려져 있다. 적확언어망각의 가장 흔한 징후 중 하나는 부분적인 기억이다. 예를 들면, 사람들은 어떤 단어가 특정 문자로 시작한다는 것을 알거나, 심지어 그 단어가 가진 음절의 개수에 대해 확신할지도 모르지만, 나머지는 기억하지 못할 수 있다. 때때로, 비슷한 소리의 단어들이 떠오른다.

왜 적확언어망각이 일어나는지에 대해서는 몇 가지 이론들이 있다. 첫 번째 이론은 적확언어망각은 목표 단어가 기억 속에서 완전히 활성화되지 않을 때 일어난다고 주장한다. 이것은 머릿속에서 목표 단어를 촉발하기 위해 일반적으로 사용되는 모든 단서들이 존재하지 않을 때 발생할 수 있다. 또 다른 이론은 비슷한 소리의 단어들에 대한 기억이 어떤 사람이 기억해 내려고 노력하는 그 단어에 대한 기억을 막는다고 주장한다. 마지막 이론은 적확언어망각은 머릿속에서 어떤 단어의 소리에 대한 기억이 그것의 의미에 대한 기억으로부터 단절될 때 일어난다고 주장한다.

적확언어망각이 기억에 미치는 영향에 대해서는 연구자들의 의견이 나누어진다. 몇몇은 애를 쓰다가 기억을 되찾는 것이 기억을 상기시키는 능력을 강화한다고 믿는 반면, 다른 사람들은 이 과정이 적확언어망각이 다시 일어날 가능성을 높인다고 생각한다.

허끝에 맴도는 단어가 있다는 것은 짜증스러울 수도 있겠지만, 그것이 당신에게 일어난다고 해도 걱정할 필요는 없다. 그것은 자연스러운 현상이고, 연구자들은 그것이 전 세계적으로 다른 언어들을 사용하는 사람들에게 흔하다는 것을 발견했다. 그것은 당신의 뇌나 기억에 문제가 있다는 것을 의미하지 않으니, 적확언어망각 때문에 스트레스 받지 마라!

구문 해설

[10행] There are several theories **as to** [*why* lethologica occurs].
▶ as to: ~에 관해서는
▶ why가 이끄는 절은 전치사 to의 목적어로 쓰인 간접의문문으로,「의문사 + 주어 + 동사」의 어순

[12행] This could happen when **not all** the cues [normally *used* **to trigger** the target word in one's mind] are present.
▶ not all: 모두 ~인 것은 아니다 (부분 부정)
▶ normally used 이하는 the cues를 수식하는 과거분사구
▶ to trigger는 목적을 나타내는 부사적 용법의 to부정사

[15행] ... when the memory of a word's sound becomes disconnected from **that** of its meaning in the mind.
▶ that은 앞에 언급된 the memory를 가리킴

[18행] Some believe [**that** *struggling* but then *retrieving* a memory strengthens one's ability to recall it], while others think that this process makes **it** more likely *for lethologica* **to happen** again.
▶ that이 이끄는 명사절 안에서 동명사구인 struggling ... memory가 주어로 쓰임
▶ it은 가목적어, to happen 이하가 진목적어이며, for lethologica는 to happen의 의미상의 주어

READING 2   p. 74~75

WORD FOCUS   refuse

accept 받아들이다 / agree 동의하다 / consent 동의하다

WORD CHECK

1. majority   2. support   3. common sense
4. notice   5. estimate
▶ generally: usually or most of the time

정답

1. d   2. It is the assumption that most other people have the same opinions we do.   3. d   4. c   5. b   6. c, e

해석

당신이 재미있게 본 영화에 대한 부정적인 평을 보고 놀란 적이 있는가? 이 놀라움은 허위 합의 효과에 의해 설명될 수 있다. 그것은 대부분의 다른 사람들이 우리와 동일한 의견을 가지고 있다는 추정이다.

많은 실험들이 허위 합의 효과가 사실이라는 것을 증명했다. 한 연구에서, 연구원들은 피실험자들에게 앞뒤로 메고 다니는 광고판을 착용한 채로 30분 동안 교정을 걸어 다니는 것에 동의할 것인지 물었다. 피실험자들은 또한 얼마나 많은 사람들이 그 광고판을 가지고 다니는 것에 동의하거나 거부할지 추측해보도록 요구받았다. 평균적으로, 광고판을 가지고 다니는 것에 동의한 사람들과 거부한 사람들 모두 대다수의 다른 사람들이 자신이 했던 것과 같은 선택을 할 것이라고 추측했다.

허위 합의 효과에는 세 가지 주된 이유가 있다. 첫째, 우리는 일반적으로 다른 사람들이 어떻게 생각하는지를 우리의 친구들이나 가족의 의견에 근거하여 예측하는데, 그들의 생각은 우리의 것과 비슷할 가능성이 높다. 둘째, 다른 사람들이 우리처럼 생각한다고 믿는 것은 우리 스스로에 대해 좋게 느끼게 한다. 마지막으로, 우리는 다른 사람들의 의견이 우리의 것과 같을 때 그것들을 알아차리고 주의를 기울일 가능성이 더 높다.

우리가 확고하게 가지고 있는 신념에 관해서라면 허위 합의 효과는 더 강력해진다. 예를 들어, 당신이 어떤 법이 당신 동네의 범죄를 줄이는 데 도움이 된다고 절대적으로 확신한다면, 당신은 이웃의 대부분 사람들 역시 그 법을 지지할 것이라고 믿을 가능성이 매우 높다.

당신은 허위 합의 효과가 사실이라고 생각하는가? 아니면 그것을 의심하는가? 당신은 다른 사람들도 당신과 같은 의견을 가지고 있다고 생각할지도 모른다. 만약 그렇다면, 당신은 바로 지금 허위 합의 효과를 경험하고 있을지도 모른다! 따라서, 모든 사람이 같은 의견을 공유하는 것은 아니라는 것을 기억하도록 해라, 심지어 그것이 상식처럼 보일 때에도 말이다!

구문 해설

4행 It is the assumption **that** most other people have the same opinions we *do*.
▶ that이 이끄는 절은 the assumption과 동격 관계
▶ do는 반복을 피하기 위해 동사 have를 대신해 쓰인 대동사

7행 In one study, researchers asked subjects **if** they would agree … *while wearing* a sandwich board with an advertisement.
▶ if: ~인지 아닌지
▶ while wearing 이하는 접속사가 생략되지 않은 분사구문

10행 On average, **both** *those* [*who* agreed to carry the board] **and** *those* [*who* refused (to carry the board)] estimated [**that** the majority of others would make the same choice they did].
▶ both A and B: A와 B 둘 다
▶ those who: ~한 사람들
▶ that 이하는 동사 estimated의 목적어 역할

13행 First, we predict [**how** others think] generally *based on* opinions of our friends and family, **whose** beliefs are likely to be similar to ours.
▶ how … think는 간접의문문으로 「의문사 + 주어 + 동사」의 어순
▶ based on: ~에 근거하여
▶ whose는 계속적 용법의 관계대명사 (= and their)

WORD REVIEW TEST

UNIT 13
p. 76
1. c   2. b   3. c   4. c   5. a   6. b   7. a   8. c
9. d   10. c   11. opposite   12. organism   13. specific
14. unpleasant

UNIT 14
p. 77
1. d   2. a   3. c   4. d   5. a   6. b   7. c   8. a
9. a   10. d   11. 2   12. 4

UNIT 15.
History

READING 1
p. 78~79

WORD FOCUS   relationship

a close relationship 친밀한 관계 / a healthy relationship 건전한 관계 / build a relationship 관계를 맺다 / end a relationship 관계를 끝내다, 헤어지다

WORD CHECK

1. colony   2. rule   3. violence   4. independence
5. spin
▶ unfair: not right or fair; without equal opportunity

정답

1. d   2. It was spun into cloth by steam-powered machines.   3. a   4. d   5. c   6. rule, cotton, cloth, peaceful, wheel

해석

영국은 18세기부터 20세기 중반까지 인도를 식민지로 지배했다. 영국의 식민지로서 인도 사람들은 많은 고통을 겪었다. 인도인들은 자신의 나라에서 거의 아무런 힘이 없었다.

이 불공평한 관계의 한 예가 목화 산업이었다. 인도인들은 목화를 재배하고 따기 위해 열심히 일했다. 수확을 마치면 목화는 영국으로 수송되었고, 그곳에서 증기 동력 기계에 의해 천으로 지어졌다. 그런 다음 그 천은 다시 인도로 선적되어 그곳에서 팔렸다. 목화는 값이 쌌지만, 천은 비쌌다. 대부분의 인도인은 자신들의 목화로 만들어진 천을 살 여력이 안 됐다!

20세기 중반에 이르러 대부분의 인도인들은 영국의 지배로부터 자유로워지기를 원했다. 그 당시 많은 독립 단체들이 결성되었다. 이 단체 중 일부는 자신들의 투쟁 과정에서 폭력 사용을 반대했다. 그들의 평화적 운동을 위해 선택된 상징물이 면을 짜는 물레인 차르카였다.

영국에 대한 저항의 수단으로, 비폭력 운동의 지도자 간디는 새로운 종류의 물레를 사용하여 스스로 옷을 만들었다. 이 새 기계는 모두가 살 수 있을 만큼 쌌고, 이곳저곳으로 갖고 다닐 수 있을 만큼 작았다. 간디는 인도인들에게 그것을 사용하는 법을 가르쳤고 그것의 사용을 독려했다. 이 기계는 많은 인기를 얻게 되었고, 인도인들은 자신들이 어디에 있든 면을 짤 수 있었다. 그들은 종종 이 기계를 영국인들이 볼 수 있는 공공장소에서 사용하곤 했다.

자신들의 천을 지어냄으로써 인도인들은 자신들의 경제와 미래를 스스로 관리할 수 있다는 것을 보여 주었다. 그들은 영국에 의존할 필요가 없었다. 그들은 무기에 의존할 필요도 없었다. 대신 그들은 평화적으로 독립을 쟁취하는 것을 택했다.

7행　..., it was shipped to England, **where** it was spun into cloth by steam-powered machines.

　▶ where은 계속적 용법의 관계부사 (= and there)

16행　This new machine was **cheap enough** for everyone **to buy** and **small enough to carry** from place to place.

　▶ 형용사 + enough + to-v: ~할 만큼 충분히 …한

19행　..., and Indians were able to spin cotton **wherever** they were.

　▶ wherever: 어디에 ~하든지 (= no matter where)

24행　**Nor** did they need to depend on weapons.

　▶ 부정어 Nor가 문장 맨 앞으로 나오면서 주어와 동사가 도치됨

READING 2　TOEFL　　　p. 80~81

정답

1. d　2. the third square　3. c　4. d　5. c　6. b, e, f

해석

미국의 노예 제도

　1600년대에 북미의 많은 유럽 정착민들은 농장에서 담배, 설탕, 목화를 재배하여 생계를 유지했다. 이 농장들은 남부에서 가장 흔했다. 단돈 27달러에 그곳의 농장주들은 아프리카 노예를 살 수 있었다. 그들은 노예를 두되 노동의 대가로 한 푼도 주지 않음으로써 많은 돈을 벌었다.

　200년이 넘도록, 해마다 수천 명의 노예가 아프리카에서 배로 실려 와 노예 시장에서 팔렸다. 1807년에 미국 정부는 노예 거래를 끝내기 위한 노력으로 노예 수입 금지 법안을 통과시켰다. 안타깝게도 이 법은 실제로 지켜지지 않았고, 노예 상인들은 계속해서 노예를 미국으로 데려왔다. 1860년경에는 남부에 약 400만 명의 노예가 있었다.

　노예들의 삶은 굉장히 힘들었다. 그들은 오랜 시간 매우 고된 일을 했다. 그들은 주인의 소유물이었다. 그들이 아이를 낳으면 아이들 또한 농장주의 소유가 되었다. 이 아이들은 태어나는 순간부터 그들이 죽는 날까지 노예였다. 그러한 체제 속에서 노예 제도는 결코 끝나지 않을 것 같았다.

　노예의 끔찍한 삶에도 불구하고 농장을 탈출하려고 시도하는 이들은 거의 없었다. 도주는 굉장히 위험한 일이었고 성공한 사람이 거의 없었다. 노예 주인들은 개를 이용하여 그들을 추적했다. 도망자가 잡히면 그 사람은 심하게 매를 맞거나 심지어는 다른 노예들의 본보기로서 죽임을 당했다.

　자유로워지기 위해, 도망친 노예는 캐나다에 도달하기 위해 수백 마일을 가야 했는데, 그곳에서는 노예 제도가 불법이었다. 그들은 몰래 이동해야 했고, 그렇지 않으면 경찰에 잡혀 농장으로 되돌려 보내졌다. 그러나 음식과 숨을 곳을 제공함으로써 도망자들을 도운 지하 철도라 불리는 소규모 비밀 조직이 있었다. 길고 위험한 여정이었지만, 일부 노예들은 자유를 얻는 데 성공했다.

4행　They made fortunes **by**
　┌ **keeping** slaves
　　and
　└ *not paying* them ....

　▶ by v-ing: ~함으로써

　▶ 동명사의 부정은 동명사 앞에 not을 씀

11행　These children were slaves **from** the moment [(*when*) they were born] **till** the day [(*when*) they died].

　▶ from A till B: A부터 B까지

　▶ 선행사인 the moment와 the day 뒤에 시간을 나타내는 관계부사 when이 생략됨

14행　..., **few** tried to escape the plantations.

　▶ few: 소수, 적은 수 (부정의 의미)

22행　..., but some slaves **did** *make it to* freedom.

　▶ 조동사 do의 과거형 did를 사용하여 동사의 의미를 강조함

　▶ make it (to): 해내다, (~에) 이르다

WORD REVIEW TEST

UNIT 15　　　　p. 82

1. d　2. a　3. d　4. b　5. c　6. a　7. c　8. b
9. a　10. c　11. fortune　12. importation
13. plantation　14. industry

READING
EXPERT